# THE MIDI BOOK

## Using MIDI and Related Interfaces

### by STEVE DE FURIA with JOE SCACCIAFERRO

**FERRO TECHNOLOGIES™**

Produced by John Cerullo
Edited by Rick Mattingly
Illustrations by Steve De Furia
Art Direction by John Flannery
Cover Photo by George Mauro

Produced and Published by
Third Earth Productions, Inc.
Pompton Lakes, NJ

Exclusively Distributed by

**HLB** HAL LEONARD BOOKS

## Acknowledgment

Special thanks to Triple S Electronics
for providing technical support
as well as enthusiastic
encouragement throughout this project.

# AUTHORS' NOTES

When we started working on this project, we realized that one of the problems facing us would be anticipating what the MIDI "state-of-the-art" would be when the book was released. We didn't want to present information in a way that could make it seem dated or obsolete six months after its release. MIDI is dynamic. It is undergoing continual refinement, evolution, and modification. Rather than trying to present an engineering specification or a trendy guide to the current generation of commercially available MIDI instruments and applications, we felt a better approach would be to give you an *enduring resource* that provides a solid foundation in MIDI concepts and their musical implications. In short, we felt we should give you the ability to put MIDI to use *right now*, while providing you with the knowledge and insight to *grow with MIDI as it evolves. THE MIDI BOOK: Using MIDI and Related Interfaces* reflects this philosophy in its design.

The book is divided into three sections. **Section I** looks at interfacing in general. As you'll see, MIDI is just one particular solution to the problem of interfacing musical instruments. One problem musicians encounter when trying to learn about MIDI is that MIDI concepts don't make much sense **if you don't already understand the concepts of interfacing in general** .

If you've ever wondered about how your physical actions are translated into musical performances, how sequencers remember and replay your music, or how drum machines, sequencers, and instruments stay in time with each other, you're about to find out. You'll also learn how computer technology is employed to perform these tasks. When you have a solid understanding of interfacing concepts, you will be able to appreciate all the more what MIDI has to offer.

In **Section II** we explore and explain every aspect of MIDI interfacing. We keep focused on specific MIDI details without bogging you down with the underlying basic principles since the general details of interfacing have already been covered in the first section. Each and every message type and the four MIDI modes are defined in detail from technical, operational, and musical points of view. You'll find that this section will serve as a master reference whenever you encounter a new MIDI concept.

In the last section we show you how to put this knowledge to use *in the real world*. If you already own some MIDI gear, you may want to skip ahead to this section first. By all means, go right ahead! If any of the MIDI terminology or interfacing concepts are unclear, you can go back to the other sections for the details.

We've chosen to present applications from a practical and musical point of view. Most of the applications presented are keyboard/sequencer/drum machine oriented since at the time this was written these were the un-silent majority in the MIDI menagerie. However, as new MIDI devices appear, you'll find that the information presented here will go a long way towards helping you learn how to incorporate new toys into your MIDI system.

You'll find out how to evaluate any instrument's MIDI features (including how to interpret Implementation Charts!), how to make the appropriate connections for simple as well as sophisticated music systems, how to interface MIDI and non-MIDI devices, and much more. We've presented the applications with generic illustrations to make the point that *they are not dependent on any particular make or model of equipment*.

Speaking of illustrations, we definitely believe one picture is worth 1K words! Check out the drawings. You'll notice they contain a great deal of useful information; not only do they show the basic connections, but they also indicate other things to look out for like which connectors to use, clock rates, sync modes, channel assignment, voicing parameters, etc.

We're sure you'll find THE MIDI BOOK an invaluable tool, whether you want to use it to gain MIDI literacy, or as your first step toward MIDI mastery.

J. Scacciaferro and S. De Furia                                                                                    Spring, '86


P.S. We've gotten so much encouragement to produce more books on related topics (and we had such a good time putting this one together), we've decided to do just that! Look for more **Ferro Technologies** books in the near future covering other aspects of Music Technology.

# TABLE OF CONTENTS

## 2.0.0
## Section II:
# THE
# SIMPLE
# TRUTH
# ABOUT
# MIDI •28

## 3.0.0
## Section III:
# PRACTICAL APPLICATIONS OF MIDI INTERFACING
**•60**

# Section I:
# WHAT IS INTERFACING,
# AND WHY DO WE NEED IT?

# 1.0.0
# *What Is Interfacing and Why Do We Need It?*

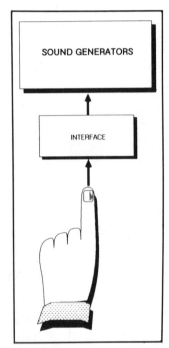

An interface is a pathway through which information flows. In musical instruments, it serves as a conduit between the performer's actions and the sound-generating components of the instrument.

Simply put, interfacing means establishing a flow of information between two or more parts of a system. The interface is the **pathway through which information flows**. With synthesizers, the interface serves as a conduit between the performer's actions and the sound-generating components of the instrument itself. Without interfacing, playing music with synthesizers would be impossible.

In an acoustic piano, the interface between the performer and the sound-generating strings is the mechanical system of keys, levers and hammers linked to specific strings. Similarly, in the first monophonic synthesizers (like Mini Moogs and ARP Odysseys), each key, knob or other control is wired directly to a specific synthesizer circuit, creating the interface between the performer and the sound-generating hardware.

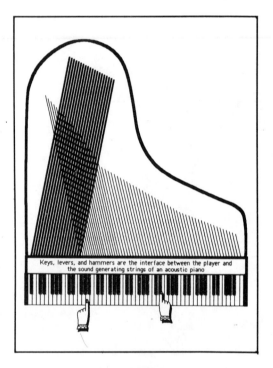

Keys, levers, and hammers are the interface between the player and the sound generating strings of an acoustic piano

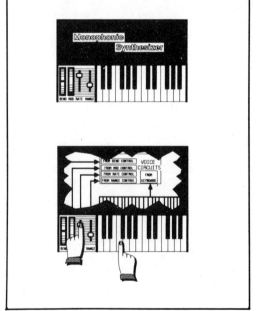

Each key, knob or other control of an older, monophonic synthesizer is wired directly to a specific circuit. These direct connections form the interface between the performance controls and the sound-generating hardware.

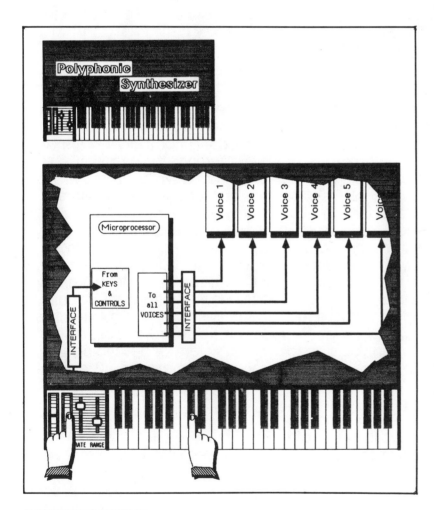

Inside every polyphonic synthesizer there is a microprocessor. Information flows from the performance controls, through the interface, to the processor. The processor transfers the information to the appropriate destination(s) via the interface.

The requirements of the two interfaces described above are relatively simple. Each performance control is permanently connected to one, and only one, part of the sound-generating system. However, the performance controls of today's typical polyphonic synthesizer cannot be permanently connected to the circuits they control. Instead, because there are many more keys than voices, the performance controls must be assigned to voices in accordance with what the player is doing. For example, on an eight-voice synthesizer, the "middle C" key might be connected to any one of eight voices, depending on how the synth is being played.

Most polyphonic synthesizers use a microprocessor (a computer on a chip) to perform these more sophisticated interfacing requirements. (Since computers use digital information, this kind of interface can be more properly referred to as a digital interface.) The interface for these instruments is a pathway that leads both to and from this internal processor. **Information is transferred from the performer to the processor, and from the processor to the sound-generating components of the synthesizer.**

What does all of this have to do with MIDI? MIDI stands for *Musical Instrument Digital Interface.* MIDI is one specific way to interface musical devices that use microprocessors. We will find that MIDI has several very special and useful properties, but before we can appreciate the significance of MIDI, we must get a better understanding of interfacing in general.

# 1.1.0 TRANSFER OF MUSICAL INFORMATION

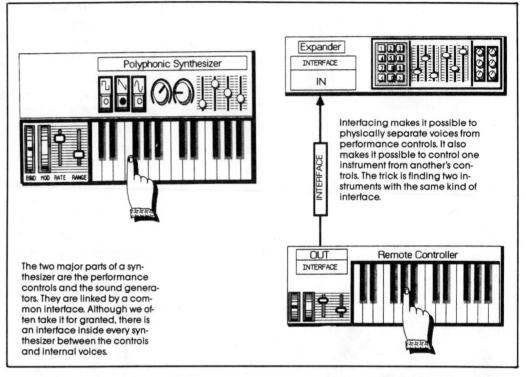

Interfacing makes it possible to physically separate voices from performance controls. It also makes it possible to control one instrument from another's controls. The trick is finding two instruments with the same kind of interface.

The two major parts of a synthesizer are the performance controls and the sound generators. They are linked by a common interface. Although we often take it for granted, there is an interface inside every synthesizer between the controls and internal voices.

First, let's see how the transfer of information is accomplished within a single instrument. You can think of your synthesizer as being made of two major parts, each with distinct functions. The first part contains all of the controls, the keyboard, knobs, switches, footpedals, etc.— everything you physically manipulate in order to play the synth. The second part contains all of the components that make up the internal voices.

Musical information is transferred between these two parts by the microprocessor. When you stop to think about it, there is no reason why the controls and sound components must both be in the same box. They could each be in a separate package, **as long as they remain connected by the interface**.

Once an interface is established between controls and sound-generating components, it makes little difference if information is transfered from a synthesizer's own controls or the controls of a different instrument. As long as both sets of controls generate information in a compatible manner, performances on either set would create music.

If both sets of controls are physically and electronically identical, then interfacing them is relatively easy. If the control sets are different, then a system for describing similar kinds of information must be worked out.

## 1.1.1 Describing Musical Events

The information transferred by an interface describes musical events. An *event* is anything done by a person that relates to either **performance** or **operation** of the instrument. Performance events include playing notes, dynamics, the movement of wheels and pedals, etc. Operational events include program changes, parameter changes, turning different modes of operation on and off, etc.

*Messages* describing these different musical events are generated by the instrument and transferred through the interface. **It is possible to describe any event with a simple message made up of two general categories of information:** *commands* and *data.*

### Commands

A command is an unambiguous order to perform a simple task. The game of Simon Says is based on the use of commands. For example, Simon says, STAND UP, is an **unambiguous order** to perform a simple action. Some commands associated with synthesizer performance and operation could be, START PLAYING, STOP PLAYING, BEND PITCH, GET A NEW SOUND.

### Data

Data is information associated with a command that defines **how much** or **which one**. For instance, in the statement Simon says, SHAKE YOUR LEFT HAND, the words left hand are data. They specify exactly what to shake. Data associated with synthesizer commands would specify things like which note to play, how far to bend a pitch, or which new sound to use.

### Messages

A message is an **explicit unit of information** that describes a single event. It is a simple statement made up of one command and any associated data. A message can describe a complete performance event such as, START PLAYING C#3, STOP PLAYING C#, BEND PITCH UP 1/2 STEP, or a complete operational event such as, CHANGE TO PRESET #32, CHANGE TO SPLIT KEYBOARD MODE, or START SEQUENCER.

Synthesizer performance and operation events are transferred through the interface as messages. Messages are made up of commands and data. A command is an unambiguous order to perform a particular task. The data associated with a particular command describes "how much" or "which one."

Generally, a message will describe a single musical event. A short musical phrase would require many messages to be transferred through the interface.

### Messages

|  | Commands | Data |
|---|---|---|
| Performance | NOTE ON | E4 |
| | NOTE OFF | Bb 3 |
| | BEND PITCH | Up Minor Third |
| | CHANGE MOD AMOUNT | 50% |
| | SUSTAIN PEDAL | Down |
| Operation | CHANGE MODE | Unison |
| | CHANGE ATTACK | 10% |
| | CHANGE RELEASE | 75% |
| | CHANGE PRESET | #14 |
| | CHANGE FM RATIO | 5/1 |
| | CHANGE FILTER Fc | 1760 Hz |
| | CHANGE MOD RATE | 5 Hz |

## 1.2.0 GETTING THE MESSAGE

Messages (made up of commands and data) describing events are generated by playing the keyboard, or otherwise manipulating the controls of the instrument. These messages flow through the interface. Eventually they arrive at the sound generators, and we hear music. How is this accomplished?

One of the many jobs of the microprocessor is to **interpret** and **transfer** these messages. The microprocessor acts like a Station Master in a busy train station. The interface is like the Inbound and Outbound tracks, and the messages are contained in cars traveling along those tracks.

## 1.2.1 Internal Messages

There are tracks leading from each performance control. They all merge together into one Inbound track that leads to the microprocessor. Every physical action sends a car down the tracks. Each car contains a message describing the event that started it.

As the instrument is played, these cars travel the Inbound track to the microprocessor. They arrive in the order that they were played. At the end of the line, the Station Master checks each car (one at a time). The Station Master must read the message and transfer it to a new car on the appropriate Outbound track. The Outbound car leaves the station, and the message arrives at the necessary synthesizer circuit (where it is acted upon).

There are specific rules (called algorithims) that are used to determine how messages are transferred to internal voices. On most synthesizers, these rules can be changed by selecting different operational modes. For example, if the synthesizer has a UNISON mode, the Station Master would assign the same note to all voices. If more than one note were played at a time, he would have to ignore the extra notes according to the rules that describe the UNISON mode. We will learn in Section II how MIDI instruments can take advantage of different voice-assignment modes.

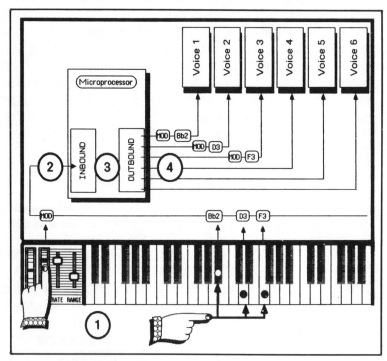

The microprocessor acts like a Station Master in a busy train station. The interface is like the Inbound and Outbound tracks. Messages travel through the interface like cars on the tracks.

Here's how messages are generated and transferred to internal voices:

1. The performer plays a B-flat triad and moves the MOD wheel. These events generate a series of performance messages.

2. The messages travel the Inbound track of the interface to the microprocessor.

3. The processor, acting like a Station Master, transfers the messages to the Outbound tracks of the interface.

4. Each note message is sent to a different voice, producing the chord. The MOD wheel message is sent simultaneously to each voice.

The microprocessor is kept quite busy dealing with the flow of messages. It is essential to understand that this transfer is not instantaneous. **It takes a certain amount of time for the messages to travel, be interpreted, and be acted upon.** The times involved will vary from instrument to instrument.

## 1.2.2 External Messages

So far, we have only been concerned with performances that originate on the same instrument that will play them. Once an interface is established between controls and hardware, **it doesn't matter if the messages originate on an instrument's own controls or not**.

In our train station, the Inbound and Outbound tracks dealt with only internal messages. We'll call those Local tracks. They handle messages coming from or going to internal hardware. Let's open our station up to the outside world by adding Express tracks. The Inbound Express carries messages that originate outside of the instrument. The Outbound Express carries messages that are going to an external instrument.

This increases the work that the Station Master must perform. Not only does the microprocessor have to take care of messages coming in on the Inbound Local line, but also it has to watch for Inbound Express messages as well. Since the Express line is connected to an external instrument, the processor has no way of knowing when a message might come along.

What happens if a Local and Express message arrive at the same time? Usually, the processor will deal with Express messages first. This is because it can control the flow of internal messages, but has no say in the flow of external ones.

When a message arrives from another instrument (via the Inbound Express track), the Station Master stops everything else, reads and transfers the message to the appropriate Outbound track, and goes back to what he was doing before the message arrived.

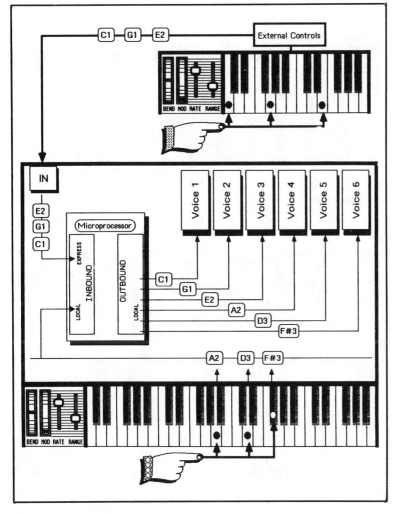

Messages originating from an external instrument arrive via the Inbound Express. The Station Master must handle both these messages and those arriving on the Inbound Local.

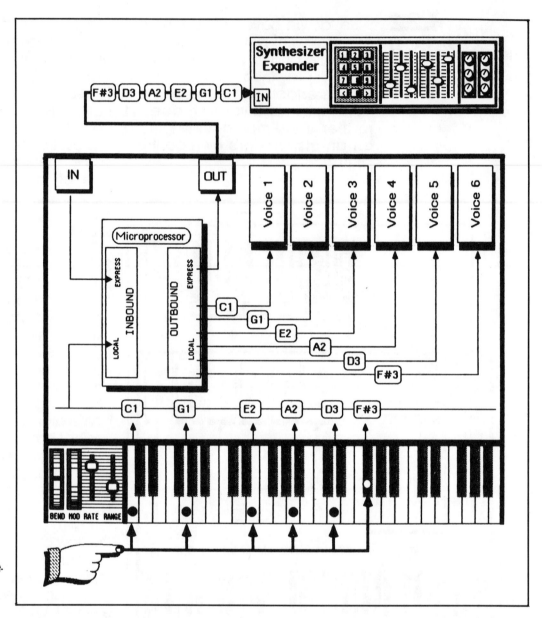

Messages originating from internal controls can be sent to an external instrument via the interface. In this case, our Station Master must duplicate Inbound messages and transfer them to both Outbound tracks. The messages routed to Outbound Local go to internal voices. Messages routed to Outbound Express leave the instrument to control external devices.

If an instrument can receive messages from external instruments, it would make sense for it to be able to send messages to external instruments as well. This means that we have to add an Outbound Express track to the station. We'll also have to give the Station Master a pay raise, as we've just made his job even more complex. Not only does the microprocessor have to handle messages from Inbound Local or Inbound Express tracks, but also it must be able to transfer them to either Outbound Local or Outbound Express tracks. Since the trains contain messages, not people, the messages can be duplicated and transferred to both Local and Express Outbound tracks at the same time. **This makes it possible for two instruments to play the same thing at the same time**.

When messages are transferred to the Outbound Express tracks they will arrive in another musical instrument's "station." The microprocessor in that instrument must then interpret the messages and transfer them to its appropriate Outbound tracks.

## 1.2.3 Summary of Interfacing Concepts

Here is a summary of how an interface transfers information between the player and the sound-generating components of polyphonic synthesizers.

1. The player's physical actions, called events, generate messages. These messages (made up of commands and data), can describe any event. These include such performance events as keys being played, movements of the bender, and dynamics, as well as such operational events as program changes, starting and stopping sequencers, and changing an instrument's mode of operation.

2. The messages are transferred through the input of the interface (the Inbound tracks) to the instrument's internal microprocessor. The messages can originate from an instrument's own controls, or they can come from another instrument.

3. The microprocessor interprets these messages as they arrive. Messages are handled one at a time. The processor must follow a strict set of rules that describes how messages are to be routed to various internal voices.

4. After they have been interpreted, they are transferred to the output of the interface (Outbound tracks) where they are sent to the appropriate sound-generating components of the instrument, or to the microprocessor of another instrument.

5. The process of interpreting and transferring messages is not instantaneous. There is always a slight delay between the occurrence of an event and the generation of sound by the synthesizer.

## 1.3.0 HOW THINGS WORK IN THE REAL WORLD

The first step in interfacing is the **generation of messages**. How are musical events transformed into messages in the first place? Every time you play a key, twist a knob or otherwise manipulate an instrument's controls, electronic signals are generated. The signals are sent through the interface to the microprocessor. The physical connection between the controls and the processor are simply a set of electrical connections called *busses*. They act like the tracks in our railway station. **Traveling these connections are electronic signals that contain the information that makes up the messages**. How can electronic signals be used to carry information?

There are two common ways to use electricity to carry information. You've undoubtedly heard of them both: analog and digital. The distinction between these two types of signals is important to musicians these days, so we thought we'd take the time to explain the difference.

## 1.3.1 Analog and Digital Information

An *analog signal* is one that can have an unlimited number of values between minimum and maximum limits. A *digital signal* is one that can have any one of a limited number of values. One of the most obvious examples of the difference between analog and digital is in the way we tell time.

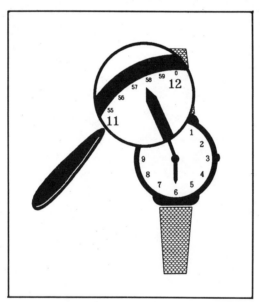

Analog information can convey an unlimited number of values between an upper and lower limit. The minute hand of this watch can convey an infinite number of time values between 6:57 and 6:58, but exactly what time is it?

### Analog

An analog clock has hands that smoothly sweep across its face. The minute hand displays time as a continuously changing value. At any given time, the hand can be in one of an unlimited number of positions between a minimum and maximum value (the 60 minutes of an hour). An advantage to this analog method of conveying information is that it can show **any possible value within the overall limits**. A disadvantage is that it is **very hard to accurately transfer, store and reproduce these values**. When the hand is in between 6:57 and 6:58, exactly what time is it? There is much room for error because of the unlimited number of possible values the information can have.

The clock uses the position of its hands to represent analog information. Analog information is conveyed electronically by the **strength or level of a signal**.

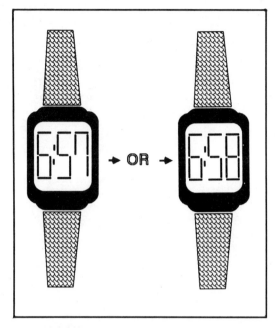

Digital information can convey one of a limited number of known values. This watch can show no time value between 6:57 and 6:58.

The digital clock has a numerical readout that changes once every minute. The minute counter on the digital clock displays time as a discrete series of values. At any given time, the counter can be one of a limited number of values (0 thru 59). An advantage of digital information is that it is **easy to transfer, store and reproduce**. There can be little doubt about the time; according to the digital clock it's either 6:57 or 6:58, and nothing in between. The disadvantage of such information is that there is **always a limit to how many possible values can be represented**.

This clock uses a series of numbers to represent information digitally. Digital information is conveyed electronically with binary code (see below).

Before microprocessors became the central element of synthesizer design, analog signals were used to interface insruments. The most common was Control Voltage, or CV. To connect such an instrument (like an Arp 2600) to a digital interface, its **analog signals must be converted to digital ones**.

## 1.3.2 Sending Musical Messages

Manipulating the controls of a synthesizer generates various signals. Some are digital, and some are analog. These signals will make up messages which are sent through the interface to the microprocessor.

The microprocessors inside the instrument can only manipulate digital information. A control-related signal may start out as analog, but somewhere along the way, it must be converted into digital information. We are not concerned with the conversion process. Just keep in mind that essentially all performance messages are digital when they get to the interface.

Three kinds of signals are associated with synthesizer interfacing: *control voltage (CV), triggers and gates,* and *binary code.*

Control voltage is an analog signal that was used primarily to convey variable information, such as pitch or loudness, for older synthesizers. Triggers and gates are used to provide timing information. Binary code can be used to specify any kind of information.

### Control Voltage

Before microprocessors, synthesizer interfaces relied on analog signals to carry information. Control voltage was generally used to indicate oscillator and filter frequency. The higher the voltage, the higher the pitch. The most commonly used convention was one volt of signal change for every pitch change of one octave. Control voltage signals are not used to indicate when a note was played; they only indicate its pitch.

Control voltage is no longer used with today's synthesizers, but some manufacturers still provide CV jacks to make instruments compatible with older models.

**Control Voltage**

1 VOLT/OCTAVE    1 VOLT/OCTAVE

1/12 3/12 5/12 7/12 9/12 11/12    1+5/12
0 2/12 4/12 6/12 8/12 10/12 1    2

Before digital interfacing, control voltage was used to transmit pitch information. The most typical format was 1 VOLT per OCTAVE. Each key transmits an analog signal 1/12th of a volt higher than the next lower key.

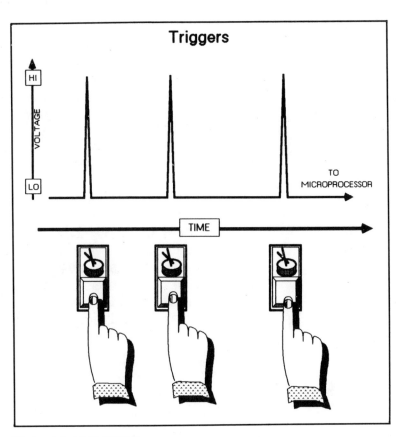

Triggers

HI

VOLTAGE

LO

TO
MICROPROCESSOR

TIME

Triggers are used to indicate
that an event has occured. For
instance, every time the snare
drum button is pushed on a
drum machine, a trigger is sent
through the interface to the
microprocessor. A trigger is just
a quick pulse of voltage. It cannot indicate what kind of event
caused it or how long the event
continued.

## Triggers

A trigger is a signal used to convey **timing information**. It is a very quick occurrence, like a flashbulb going off. Typically, a trigger is used to indicate that an **event has occurred**. It can convey **no information about what kind of event caused it or how long it continued**.

A trigger signal might be generated when you push a button to toggle a function between on and off. A series of evenly timed trigger signals could be used like a metronome to indicate a tempo, controlling the rate of an arpeggiator, for example.

13

## A gate

A gate is another signal used to indicate event timing. Like a trigger, it **cannot convey information about what kind of event has occurred**. Unlike a trigger however, it can be used to indicate **how long an event continues**. Gates work like a door buzzer. When the event begins, the buzzer goes on. It stays on as long as the event continues.

Old synthesizers used gates to indicate that a key was held down (a CV signal indicated the key's pitch). A special kind of gate signal is called a clock. It is an **evenly timed series of gates** used as a timing reference for sequencers and drum machines (see below: Keeping Time).

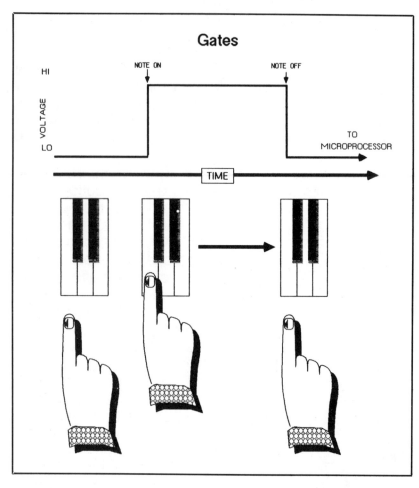

Like triggers, gates are used to indicate that an event has occured. Unlike triggers, gates indicate the duration of an event. For example, on older synthesizers a gate is transmitted when a key is pushed down. The gate remains "ON" as long as a finger is holding down the key. A gate cannot convey information about what kind of event caused it.

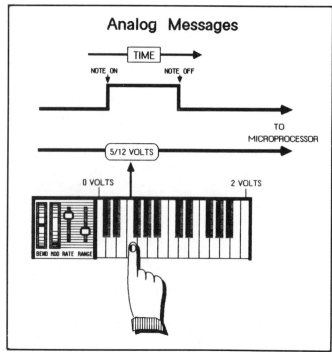

When analog control voltage is used to convey pitch information, it is also necessary to send a gate signal through the interface. The control voltage is used to specify which key is being played, and the gate specifies when the key was pressed and the duration of the note.

A clock signal is a series of evenly timed gates. Clocks are used as a timing reference by the microprocessors in sequencers and drum machines.

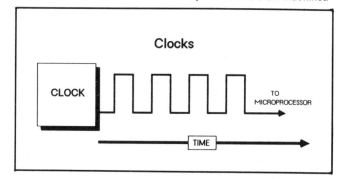

## *Binary Code*

We explained above that digital signals carry information as numbers within a limited range. How can electrical signals be used to represent numbers? One simple way would be to send a series of triggers. If you wanted to convey the number ten, send ten triggers. The number eight would be eight triggers, and so on. This might work out for small numbers, but what about very large ones? The larger the number, the more time it would take to send or receive it.

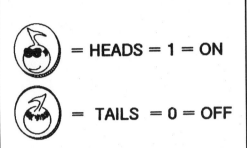

| PATTERN OF COINS | CODE | BITS |
|---|---|---|
| | = 0 = | 0 0 0 |
| | = 1 = | 0 0 1 |
| | = 2 = | 0 1 0 |
| | = 3 = | 0 1 1 |
| | = 4 = | 1 0 0 |
| | = 5 = | 1 0 1 |
| | = 6 = | 1 1 0 |
| | = 7 = | 1 1 1 |

Binary code uses a series of BITS to convey information. A bit can have one of two mutually exclusive values - HEADS or TAILS, 1 or 0, or ON or OFF.

Three coins can be arranged into eight unique patterns of heads and tails.

In order to convey numbers efficiently, it was necessary to work out a code. The code used to send digital messages is called *binary*. In theory, it is similar to Morse code. Instead of using groups of Dots and Dashes to represent words, binary code uses groups of digits, called *bits*, to represent numbers. ("Bit" is an abbreviation of the words binary digit.) A single bit can have only one of two mutually exclusive values, for example: On or Off, High or Low, One or Zero. Binary code is a digital signal that contains the actual commands or data represented as groups of binary digits.

Here's how it works: A bit must always be one of two values and never anything else. These values are equal but opposite, like Up and Down. It makes little difference what we call the values. When working with numbers, the values 1 and 0 are convenient. When working with electricity, On and Off are convenient. For this example, let's work with coins.

A short series of bits can be used to represent a large range of numbers. We'll use coins to represent single bits. The value of each bit can be either Heads or Tails - never anything else. We'll take a fixed number

| BITS | CODE | ELECTRONIC SIGNAL |
|---|---|---|
| 0 0 0 0 | = 0 | = OFF OFF OFF OFF |
| 0 0 0 1 | = 1 | = OFF OFF OFF ON |
| 0 0 1 0 | = 2 | = OFF OFF ON OFF |
| 0 0 1 1 | = 3 | = OFF OFF ON ON |
| 0 1 0 0 | = 4 | = OFF ON OFF OFF |
| 0 1 0 1 | = 5 | = OFF ON OFF ON |
| 0 1 1 0 | = 6 | = OFF ON ON OFF |
| 0 1 1 1 | = 7 | = OFF ON ON ON |
| 1 0 0 0 | = 8 | = ON OFF OFF OFF |
| 1 0 0 1 | = 9 | = ON OFF OFF ON |
| 1 0 1 0 | = 10 | = ON OFF ON OFF |
| 1 0 1 1 | = 11 | = ON OFF ON ON |
| 1 1 0 0 | = 12 | = ON ON OFF OFF |
| 1 1 0 1 | = 13 | = ON ON OFF ON |
| 1 1 1 0 | = 14 | = ON ON ON OFF |
| 1 1 1 1 | = 15 | = ON ON ON ON |

**ANATOMY OF A DIGITAL WORD**

BIT = 0 or 1

BYTE = Eight BITS

10110011

WORD = 1 or more BYTES

01011001

01101110  00011100

Bits are arranged into patterns. Each unique pattern is assigned a code number. Three bits can be arranged into 8 unique patterns, four bits into 16, eight bits into 256, and so on.

of coins and assign a number to each unique pattern of Heads and/or Tails they can be arranged in.

You can arrange **three** coins into **eight** unique patterns of Heads and Tails. **Four** coins can be arranged into any of **sixteen** different patterns. **Eight** coins could be arranged into 256 different patterns, and **sixteen** coins could be arranged into over 65,536 unique patterns.

Binary code is made up of digital *"words."* Each word contains one or more *"bytes."* Each byte contains a pattern of eight bits. Each bit can have an electrical value of On or Off (it is usually convenient to think of bits as 1's and 0's). A one-byte word could equal one of 256 different numbers.

In synthesizers and related instruments, each possible command is assigned a number. A **single-byte word can then be used to specify up to 256 different commands**. If more commands are needed, a two-byte word (16 bits) could be used to represent up to 65,536 unique commands!

Data could be represented in the same way. A one-byte word can be used to indicate one of 256 different keys, or one of 256 possible, preset sounds. Larger values can be conveyed with larger words.

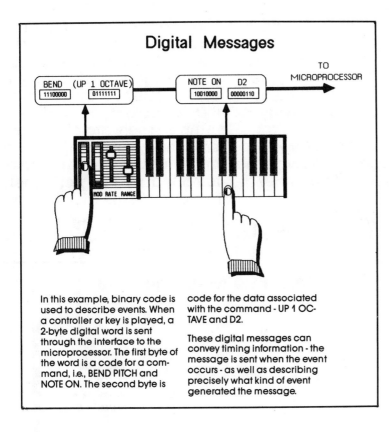

## Digital Messages

BEND (UP 1 OCTAVE)
11100000    01111111

NOTE ON    D2
10010000    00000110

TO MICROPROCESSOR

MOD RATE RANGE

In this example, binary code is used to describe events. When a controller or key is played, a 2-byte digital word is sent through the interface to the microprocessor. The first byte of the word is a code for a command, i.e., BEND PITCH and NOTE ON. The second byte is code for the data associated with the command - UP 1 OCTAVE and D2.

These digital messages can convey timing information - the message is sent when the event occurs - as well as describing precisely what kind of event generated the message.

It is possible to describe every possible musical event with binary code. Each knob, switch, key and wheel can be given a unique code number. The position of a controller can be given as one value within a limited range of numbers. When a synthesizer is designed, a list is created that contains a unique code number for every single control on the instrument. Whenever an event occurs, the code number and position of the control that has been moved are sent through the interface to the miroprocessor. The microprocessor looks up the code number and transfers the position value to the appropriate circuitry.

## 1.3.3 Receiving Musical Messages

The different kinds of devices associated with a musical interface will usually do one of two things with messages as they are received. They will either **act upon them in real time** or **store them away** for later use.

The simplest way to deal with incoming messages is to carry out the commands they contain as they arrive. This is the real time mode of operation for a synthesizer. You hit a key and hear a note. You move a knob and hear a change in sound quality. The Station Master (remember him?) reads messages as they come in and transfers them to the appropriate sound modules (where they will be acted upon).

This is a very straightforward approach to interfacing. **The order and timing of the messages is determined by the performer**. The microprocessor merely reacts to messages as they arrive.

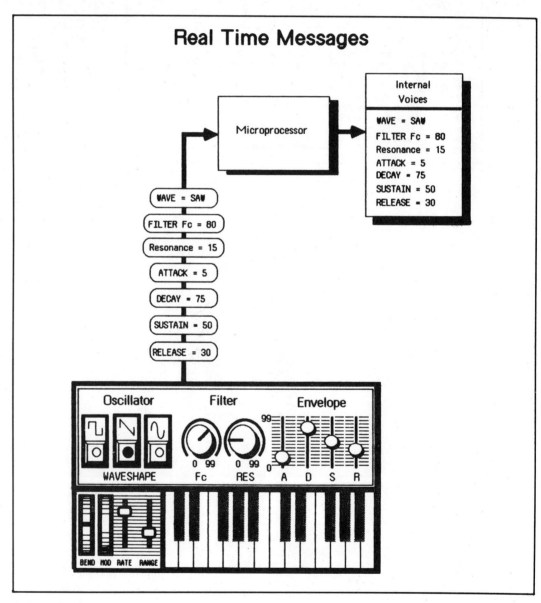

**Real Time Messages**

Microprocessor

Internal Voices

WAVE = SAW
FILTER Fc = 80
Resonance = 15
ATTACK = 5
DECAY = 75
SUSTAIN = 50
RELEASE = 30

WAVE = SAW
FILTER Fc = 80
Resonance = 15
ATTACK = 5
DECAY = 75
SUSTAIN = 50
RELEASE = 30

Oscillator    Filter    Envelope

99

0  99    0  99    0
WAVESHAPE    Fc    RES    A    D    S    R

BEND  MOD  RATE  RANGE

During performance, messages from the synthesizer's programming controls are sent directly to the internal voices by the microprocessor.

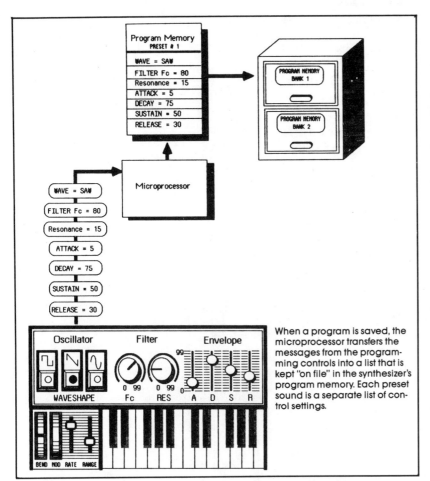

When a program is saved, the microprocessor transfers the messages from the programming controls into a list that is kept "on file" in the synthesizer's program memory. Each preset sound is a separate list of control settings.

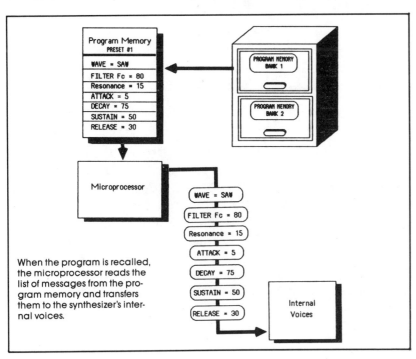

When the program is recalled, the microprocessor reads the list of messages from the program memory and transfers them to the synthesizer's internal voices.

## Keeping Records

The great advantage of defining messages with binary code is that it makes them easy to store and retrieve. All that is necessary is a place to keep a group of messages. Most synthesizers have memory hardware (called RAM). The processor can use memory-like filing cabinets to keep records of messages. The easiest kind of record to store is a simple list of messages. If the list is stored and recalled in a known order, it is possible to do some very useful things.

For example, when you create a sound on a synthesizer and save it, here's what happens: The processor reads all of the messages associated with the parameter controls and transfers this list into memory. When you recall the sound, the processor reads the list from memory and transfers the messages to the appropriate sound modules.

This method of storage works fine with preset sounds, or keyboard setups. However, if you want to store a performance, the interface must provide some way for the processor to keep track of **when the events happened**. Going back to the train station example, the Station Master would have to write down the time when each message arrived. This *timing reference* would have to be included in the list. This means that a clock must be provided for the station master.

## Keeping Time

**The microprocessor must have access to a clock in order to preserve accurately the rhythms of performance events.** We will call this the *Event Clock*. It is a series of evenly timed gates. The Event Clock is used by the processor as a timing reference. Since every time an event occurs a message is sent, **the rhythm of events can be stored as the arrival time of messages**. Here's how this is done.

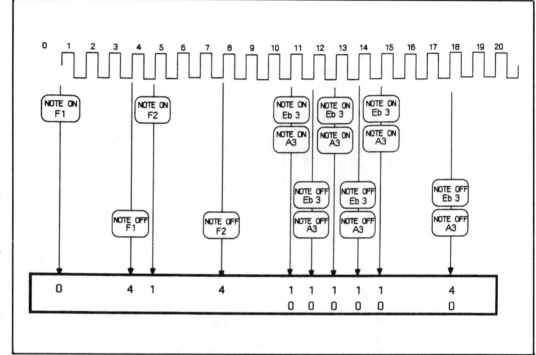

These are the counter numbers that are stored along with the performance messages. They tell the microprocessor how many clock ticks to wait before playing each message. Notice that messages must be sent when a note stops as well as when it starts. When two messages are sent at the same time, the counter number for the second message is 0, since no ticks occurred between the two messages. This is how chords can be stored.

Within the synthesizer, there is a counter that can be used by the processor. It counts the "ticks" of the Event Clock: one tick for each gate. When a message is received, the processor stores the message along with the counter number. Then it resets the counter to 0 and waits for the next message. The counter starts counting ticks again.

When the next message arrives, the message and the new counter number are added to the list. The counter is reset and the process repeats. The resulting list contains not only the list of performance messages in the order that they occurred, but the **number of clock ticks between each message**.

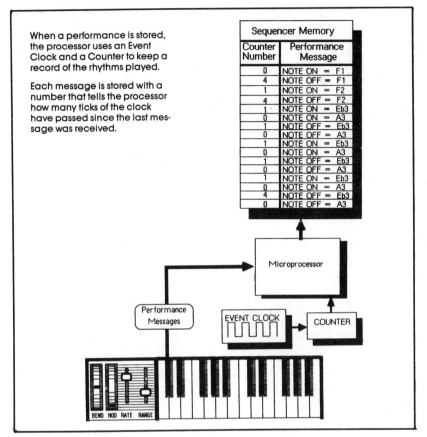

When a performance is stored, the processor uses an Event Clock and a Counter to keep a record of the rhythms played.

Each message is stored with a number that tells the processor how many ticks of the clock have passed since the last message was received.

| Sequencer Memory | |
| --- | --- |
| Counter Number | Performance Message |
| 0 | NOTE ON = F1 |
| 4 | NOTE OFF = F1 |
| 1 | NOTE ON = F2 |
| 4 | NOTE OFF = F2 |
| 1 | NOTE ON = Eb3 |
| 0 | NOTE ON = A3 |
| 0 | NOTE OFF = Eb3 |
| 0 | NOTE OFF = A3 |
| 1 | NOTE ON = Eb3 |
| 0 | NOTE ON = A3 |
| 1 | NOTE OFF = Eb3 |
| 0 | NOTE ON = A3 |
| 1 | NOTE ON = Eb3 |
| 0 | NOTE ON = A3 |
| 4 | NOTE OFF = Eb3 |
| 0 | NOTE OFF = A3 |

When the performance is recalled, the processor reads through the list, one message at a time. Using the Event Clock as a timing reference, it waits for the number of ticks stored with a message and then transfers the message to the appropriate voice. It then waits for the number of ticks stored with the next message and transfers it. This process continues until there are no more messages left to read. Slowing down or speeding up the clock speed will alter the tempo of the music as it is played back. The internal rhythms of the piece will remain constant, since there will still be the same number of ticks between each event. This is how sequencers and drum machines are able to "remember" what was played into them. They keep a list of performance messages and counter numbers.

This method of synchronization is accurate to the **nearest clock tick**. When an event occurs in between clock cycles, the counter number will be for either the click before or the click after the event. When the performance is replayed, that event will be either a little early or a little late. This source of error can be minimized by using a clock that produces the same number of ticks per beat regardless of the tempo.

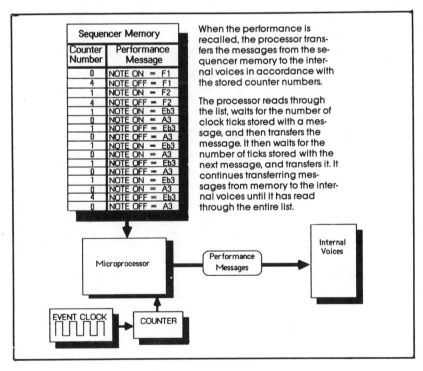

| Sequencer Memory | |
| --- | --- |
| Counter Number | Performance Message |
| 0 | NOTE ON = F1 |
| 4 | NOTE OFF = F1 |
| 1 | NOTE ON = F2 |
| 4 | NOTE OFF = F2 |
| 1 | NOTE ON = Eb3 |
| 0 | NOTE ON = A3 |
| 1 | NOTE OFF = Eb3 |
| 0 | NOTE OFF = A3 |
| 1 | NOTE ON = Eb3 |
| 0 | NOTE ON = A3 |
| 1 | NOTE OFF = Eb3 |
| 0 | NOTE OFF = A3 |
| 1 | NOTE ON = Eb3 |
| 0 | NOTE ON = A3 |
| 4 | NOTE OFF = Eb3 |
| 0 | NOTE OFF = A3 |

When the performance is recalled, the processor transfers the messages from the sequencer memory to the internal voices in accordance with the stored counter numbers.

The processor reads through the list, waits for the number of clock ticks stored with a message, and then transfers the message. It then waits for the number of ticks stored with the next message, and transfers it. It continues transferring messages from memory to the internal voices until it has read through the entire list.

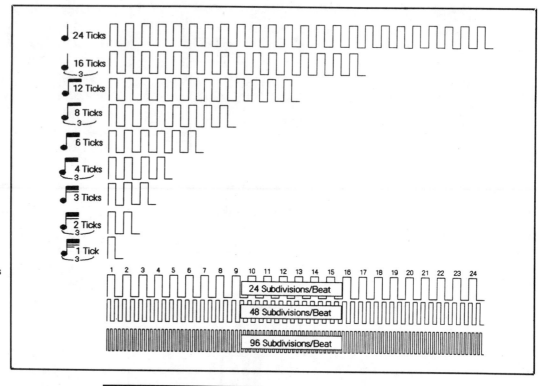

This chart shows how common rhythms fall neatly onto the ticks of a 24 subdivisions per beat Event Clock. These same rhythms would also be cleanly captured by 48 and 96 subdivisions per beat clocks as well. The number of ticks per rhythm would be twice and four times the amounts shown here.

## Subdividing Beats

The Event Clocks used by musical interfaces are really sophisticated metronomes. Instead of ticking just once per beat at a quarter-note rate, they split a beat into equal subdivisions. No matter what the tempo of such a clock, **one tick would always equal the same rhythmic value**.

Most Event Clocks subdivide a beat into 24, 48, or 96 beat divisions. These are the rhythmic equivalents to 64th-note triplets, 128th-note triplets, and 256th-note triplets. These particular beat subdivisions offer two musical advantages.

The first advantage is gained by using such relatively fast clock rates. Errors will occur if the performer can play quicker rhythms than the beat subdivision. Using such small rhythmic units ensures that the clock will always be faster than the performer. Not much music requires rhythms faster than 64th-note triplets!

The second advantage is related to the actual number of subdivisions the clock divides a beat into. The faster the rate, the more likely that an event will happen exactly on a clock tick. However, it is still possible for events to land in between ticks. Providing a quarter-note metronome to the player helps to synchronize with the Event Clock. This makes rhythms played on the beat occur on the ticks of the clock.

The particular subdivisions used by these clocks are all divisible by two's and three's. This means that any rhythm that divides a beat by two's or three's will fall on a tick. Since most music consists of quarter, eighth, sixteenth (etc.) rhythms and their triplets, these particular subdivisions will accurately "catch" most rhythms played by the performer.

## 1.4.0 COMPOUND INTERFACES

You can see now that there are really two things to consider in a musical interface.

If you want one instrument to be able to "play" others, the interface must be able to transfer messages that are sent whenever a performance or operational event occurs. If you want to synchronize the timing between two or more devices, the interface must provide an Event Clock that can be used as a timing reference. If you are using several different kinds of instruments together as a system, it is often necessary to transfer both event messages and a timing reference.

### The Event Interface

In order to transfer performance or operational information in real time between synthesizers, or between synthesizers and a sequencer, it is only necessary for the interface to exchange messages that describe these events. Performance events include depressing/releasing keys, moving controllers such as pitch or mod wheels, and using keyboard dynamics. Operational events include changing programs, altering voicing parameters, and changing voicing assignments.

Most synthesizers designed before MIDI provide only this event aspect of the interface.

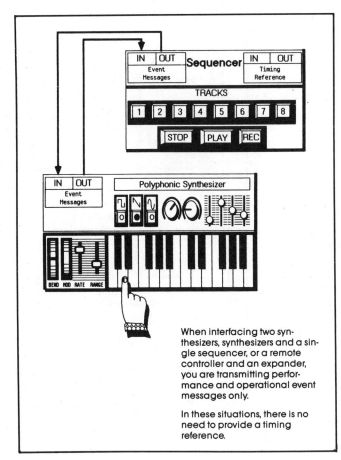

When interfacing two synthesizers, synthesizers and a single sequencer, or a remote controller and an expander, you are transmitting performance and operational event messages only.

In these situations, there is no need to provide a timing reference.

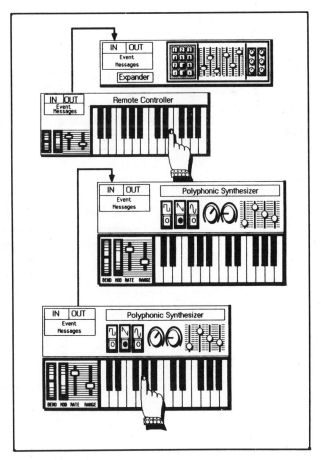

## Timing Interface

When two or more sequencers, drum machines, or arpeggiators are used together, they must be synchronized with a common Event Clock. This timing reference is used to keep the different units in time with each other. It has nothing to do with the actual notes or rhythms they may play.

In order for the timing interface to work properly, each drum machine, sequencer, etc., must be set for the same number of beat subdivisions. The Event Clock must be electronically compatible with each of these units as well (see Section III: Applications).

Most drum machines and sequencers designed before MIDI provide only this timing aspect of the interface.

## Compound Interface

There is a great deal of interest today in using various synthesizers, drum machines and sequencers together to form a composite system. In order to get the most flexibility from such a system, the interface should provide both an **event interface** and a **timing interface** to the system as a whole.

In the past, this usually required two separate sets of interface connections: one for events and one for the timing reference. A *compound interface* is one that transfers both event and timing messages between units via the same physical connection.

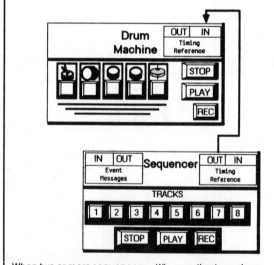

When two or more sequencers or drum machines are interfaced together, they must share a common timing reference. The interface keeps the drum and sequencer rhythms synchronized with each other. The Event Clock they share is like a metronome. It indicates where the beats (and sub-beats) fall. It carries no information about the actual notes or rhythms being performed.

When synthesizers, drum machines and sequencers are used together, it is necessary to use a compound interface. Both event messages and a timing reference must be provided. Before MIDI, this usually meant hooking up two separate sets of cables: one for event messages and one for the timing reference. The MIDI interface sends both types of information through the same cable.

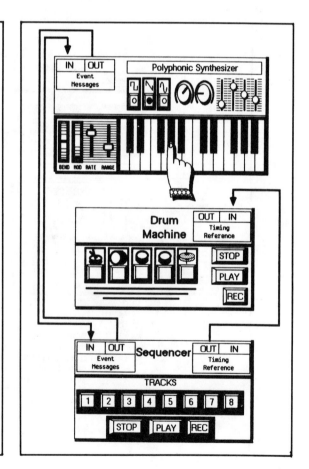

## 1.4.1 Considerations for a Compound Interface

There have been several successful compound interfaces for musical instruments before MIDI. Unfortunately, each manufacturer used an interface scheme of its own design. Because of the newness of the technology, and the vast differences in instrument design philosophy and sophistication, it was next to impossible to make unlike instruments communicate through a common event and/or timing interface.

To further complicate matters, two different approaches were taken to the actual electronic design of the interface itself. Some systems used parallel circuitry while others used serial circuitry. These two approaches to circuit design affect two crucial factors: the speed of the interface and its costs.

As we have learned, digital interface messages are made up of words. Each word contains one or more bytes. Each byte is a pattern of eight bits. A crucial factor to any interface is how quickly it can transfer digital information between instruments. The rate must be many times faster than the Event Clock. This is because, in a system with several devices interfaced together, many messages may be sent, received and processed in between ticks of the event clock. (In order for our overworked Station Master to do his job, he must be moving very much faster than a person, or persons, playing the instruments.)

The transfer of digital information is controlled by a *transmission clock*. *The rate of these clocks may vary with different instruments, but they are typically on the order of several tens of thousands of cycles per second.*

### Parallel

A *parallel interface* transmits an entire word in one transmission cycle. This allows for very speedy transfer of information, but it has some drawbacks. Parallel interfaces require expensive circuitry, which of course, makes the instruments that use them more expensive. There is also a limit to how long the physical connection between two instruments can be. Typically, the length of a connecting cable must be kept under ten feet.

### Serial

*Serial interfaces* must transfer digital information one bit at a time. This makes them generally slower than parallel interfaces (eight times slower at the same transmission rate for a one-byte word). The transmission rate of a serial interface is often given in *"Baud"* (bits per second) or *KBaud* (thousands of bits per second). However, serial interfaces are much less expensive to build, and can have physical connections with greater lengths (as much as fifty feet). This is good news to musicians with limited budgets, especially if they want to walk around the stage uninhibited by the length of the cable attaching the remote keyboard to the synthesizer rack backstage.

## 1.4.2 Real World Examples of Compound Interfaces

As synthesizers developed, so did various other peripheral devices such as drum machines and sequencers. It was not practical to build all of this equipment into one big unit, so it was necessary to develop ways of interfacing them together. Before MIDI each manufacturer introduced its own compound interface. Each of these interfaces works very well, but only with one brand of equipment.

For example, some older Oberheim, pre-MIDI instruments used a compound interface that utilized parallel circuitry. The connectors for the interface are labeled *"Computer Interface"* or *"Synthesizer Interface."* The interface carries both event messages and a timing reference. The codes used to define messages, as well as the electrical requirements of the interface circuitry are defined by Oberheim. The interface works exclusivly with Oberheim products, and therefore is not compatible with any other manufacturer's instruments.

Another example is Roland's pre MIDI compound interface, called *DCB (Digital Communications Buss)*. This is an example of a serial interface. It can transfer event messages and a timing reference between any Roland instruments equipped with a Roland DCB connector. It, too, is incompatible with instruments made by other manufacturers. The information carried by the interface and its electronic design have definitions that are unique to Roland products.

In order for different brands of equipment to work together, they must **all use one common interface**. The synthesizer industry as a whole has carefully defined a standard for interfacing musical instruments. The standard specifies the electrical requirements of the interface, the **binary codes** used to define events and a timing reference, and the **transmission rate** of these digital signals. It is the first common interface scheme to be accepted by all manufacturers of synthesizers and related equipment.

*MIDI* stands for Musical Instrument Digital Interface. It is a serial interface with a transmission rate of 31,250 bits per second (31.25 KBaud). It transfers both **event messages** and a **timing reference** as digital codes. MIDI has many unique and powerful optional features. Manufacturers may take advantage of these options if they wish.

MIDI is by no means the best or only possible musical interface. It is significant because it is the only system that can be used to interface various instruments made by different manufacturers. **It ensures that all MIDI products will be compatible with each other on some common level**. Virtually every synthesizer, drum machine and sequencer being made today has connections for MIDI interfacing built in.

# Section II:
# THE SIMPLE TRUTH
# ABOUT MIDI

# 2.0.0 The Simple Truth About MIDI

MIDI is relatively new (introduced in 1982). There is every reason to believe that using it will become second nature to all of us. . . eventually. For the time being however, there is a lot of confusion about what it can do and how to use it.

MIDI is intended to be a simple, sophisticated way of interfacing diverse musical instruments together. Much of the initial confusion associated with MIDI was caused by the fact that the majority of first-generation MIDI synthesizers, sequencers, and drum machines were not designed with MIDI in mind. The MIDI implementations on these instruments were added after the fact, and in many cases represented a limited subset of possible MIDI features. Furthermore, the manner in which MIDI features were accessed by the user on these earlier instruments were not always straight forward. The instrument designers were limited to using pre-existing controls to activate both synthesizer and MIDI functions. The newest generation of synthesizers and related gear is being designed around MIDI. They utilize more MIDI features and, where appropriate, have dedicated controls for MIDI functions. The function and nature of digital interfacing in general is another source of confusion. Here we all are, trying to keep up with how individual instruments work and now we have to start learning how to connect them together. Once they are connected properly, then what? What advantages does MIDI offer to the performer, composer or producer?

The simple truth about MIDI is this:

MIDI can be a powerful and efficient new tool for musicians who take the time to learn how to use it. If you don't understand it, MIDI can be a frustrating waste of time.

MIDI is not going to go away. More and more musical goodies will be designed to take advantage of what MIDI has to offer. As a musician looking towards the 1990's, you have three choices:

1. SINK: Forget about the whole thing. Never use more than one instrument at a time, or take up painting.

2. FLOAT: Learn just enough to get by. If you get into trouble you can pay other people to make things work for you.

3. SWIM: Jump right in and learn everything you can about MIDI. If you're reading this, you must be a swimmer. Good for you! Ask questions. Study your instruments. READ THE MANUALS. Hang in there. It will pay off eventually. You will find that MIDI will expand your horizons as a performer, composer or producer. Besides, you might be able to make a little cash from the floaters. . . .

## 2.1.0 MIDI DEFINED

MIDI is a serial interface that operates at 31.25 KBaud. Both event messages and timing reference are transmitted as digital words of binary code. They are carried via a single cable between instruments.

MIDI messages are commands and data used by the instruments to specify a variety of performance and operation events. There are five types of MIDI messages.

1. *Channel Voice Messages*: are used to convey all events associated with performance. These messages can be assigned to **sixteen independent polyphonic channels**.

2. *Channel Mode Messages*: are used to specify **channel** and **voice assignments** on instruments that incorporate such features into their MIDI design.

3. *System Common Messages*: are available to all instruments in a system. They are used to specify **preset songs** and **beat locations** within those songs.

4. *System Real Time Messages*: are also available to all of the units in a system. They are used to convey **timing reference** information.

5. *System Exclusive Messages*: These messages are used to carry information that is intended for a **specific brand or model of instrument**.

## 2.1.1 MIDI Interface Electronics

MIDI instruments are interfaced via the MIDI ports. A single three-conductor cable is required. The terminations may either be a *5-pin DIN connector*, or a *3-pin Amphenol connector*. The DIN connector seems to be the most widely used at this time.

Any instrument that has MIDI, has an internal microprocessor. Unfortunately, microprocessors are sensitive to noise or transients in AC power sources. Here are some precautions you can take to protect your investment in expensive musical equipment:

Use a *line filter* to protect your MIDI instruments from line noise caused by light dimmers and electric motors. A noisy power source can cause such problems as **data errors** and **erratic system behavior**.

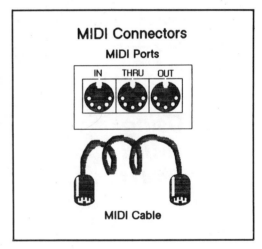

**MIDI Connectors**

MIDI Ports

IN    THRU    OUT

MIDI Cable

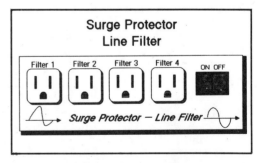

**Surge Protector Line Filter**

Filter 1  Filter 2  Filter 3  Filter 4   ON  OFF

*Surge Protector — Line Filter*

A surge protector line filter can protect your valuable MIDI instruments from AC related problems. If you use one with multiple outlets, don't plug anything but MIDI instruments or other microprocessor-based equipment into it. Don't plug amplifiers or lighting equipment into the surge protector with your MIDI gear.

29

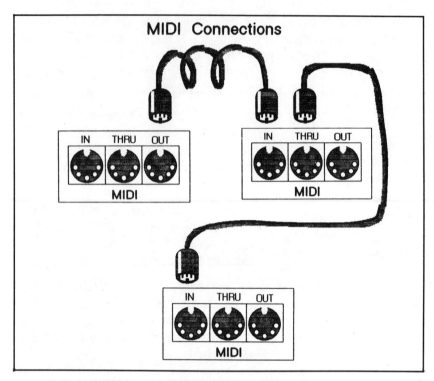

**MIDI Connections**

These are the only valid MIDI connections you can make. NEVER connect a MIDI OUT port to a THRU port or another OUT port. NEVER connect any MIDI port to a non-MIDI port with the same kind of connector. ALWAYS turn the power off an instrument BEFORE you connect or disconnect its MIDI ports.

Use a *surge suppressor* to protect your MIDI instruments from "spikes" caused by other equipment being turned on and off, power outages, etc. Surges can cause **data** or **RAM errors**, and also **damage solid state components** or the microprocessor itself.

A single unit that combines both line filters and surge protection for four instruments can be purchased for about $65.00. It's worth it.

Before connecting MIDI devices together, make sure that their **power is off**. Check your connections before you turn the instruments on. The IN port should only be connected to either an OUT or THRU port. The OUT port should only be connected to an IN port. **An improper connection, or disconnecting cables with the instruments on, can damage solid state components in the MIDI circuitry.**

---

### 2.1.2 Using MIDI Ports

The MIDI connections are called *ports*. They do not carry audio information. They are used to transmit and receive MIDI messages only. The three ports allow a great deal of flexibility when making up a system. Each port has a different function.

---

### The OUT Port

All messages that originate from an instrument's keyboard or other onboard controls are transmitted from the MIDI OUT port.

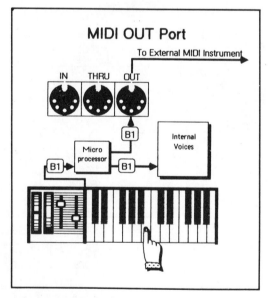

**MIDI OUT Port**

Messages that originate from an instrument's keyboard or other controls are sent to the MIDI OUT port, as well as the internal voices.

## The IN Port

Messages arriving at the MIDI IN port are routed to the instrument's internal sound-generating hardware. A synthesizer will respond to messages from its IN port as though they originated on its own keyboard.

## The THRU Port

Many instruments have a MIDI THRU port. It transmits an exact duplicate of messages arriving at the IN port. The THRU port does not carry any messages originating from the instrument's own keyboard. It is used to pass externally generated MIDI messages on to an additional instrument.

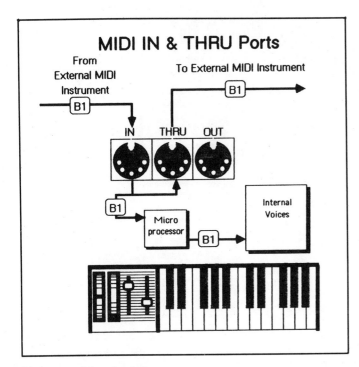

Messages arriving at an instrument's MIDI IN port are routed to the internal voices. The instrument will respond to these messages as though they originated from its own controls.

The THRU port transmits an exact duplicate of all messages arriving via the IN port. This makes it possible to pass the messages on to additional instruments. The THRU port does not carry messages originating from the instrument's own controls.

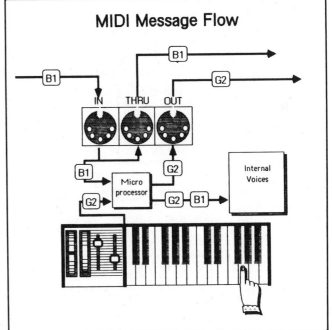

An instrument can be controlled simultaneously by its own keyboard and by messages arriving via the IN port.

Notice that the THRU and OUT ports do NOT carry the same messages.

## 2.1.3 Examples of MIDI Connections

The following diagrams illustrate several of the common ways of interfacing synthesizers using the three MIDI ports.

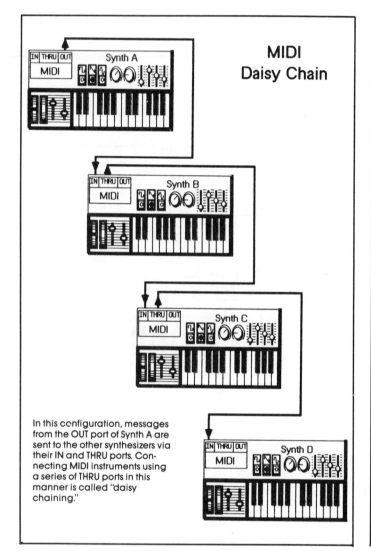

**MIDI Daisy Chain**

In this configuration, messages from the OUT port of Synth A are sent to the other synthesizers via their IN and THRU ports. Connecting MIDI instruments using a series of THRU ports in this manner is called "daisy chaining."

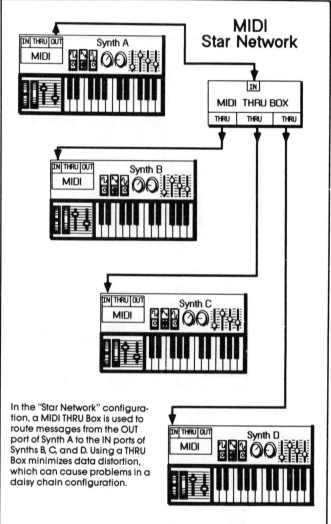

**MIDI Star Network**

In the "Star Network" configuration, a MIDI THRU Box is used to route messages from the OUT port of Synth A to the IN ports of Synths B, C, and D. Using a THRU Box minimizes data distortion, which can cause problems in a daisy chain configuration.

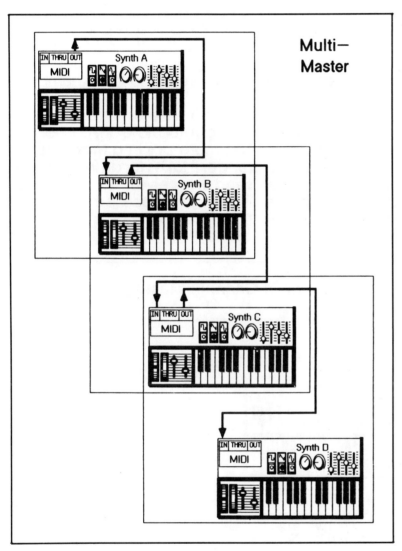

In this configuration, Synth A
sends messages only to Synth B,
Syth B sends messages only to
Synth C, and Synth C sends
messages only to Synth D.

## 2.2.0 THE MIDI MESSAGES

Performance and operation events are described with MIDI messages. Each message describes a **single event**. All MIDI messages are made up of a series of words of binary code. The first word of any message is called the *status word*. It contains the command portion of the message. The status word of all channel messages also contains a *MIDI channel number*. **An instrument's MIDI Mode determines whether or not the channel number is ignored or acted upon** (see below).

We have included diagrams showing you the exact contents of most MIDI messages. We use the following format in our definitions: The COMMAND portion of a message is spelled totally in upper-case letters. The Data portion is spelled in upper and lower case. A slash ("/") is used to separate COMMANDs and Data. For example, NOTE ON/Key Number/Attack Velocity, is a complete MIDI message. We will often refer to a message with just its COMMAND name, i.e., a NOTE ON message.

We have also included the actual binary code used for each message. You probably don't care what the binary code for a particular message is, but you should at least be aware of the large number of bits than an instrument must send and receive every time you push a key down (or move any control, etc.). **The more bits in a message, the longer it takes for an instrument to send or receive it**. Remember, MIDI is a serial interface. Its messages are transferred between units one bit at a time.

MIDI messages are made up of groups of eight-bit words. The first word of a message is called a Status word. It may be followed by one or more Data words. The number of words in each particular message is defined by the MIDI specification.

This example shows the actual binary codes, in the order that they are sent, when a D1 key is pushed down - generating a NOTE ON message. It is not important that you know these codes. However, it is important that you realize that this kind of information is transmitted (one bit at a time) every time a key is played or any other control is moved.

If you are really interested, here is the format MIDI instruments use that allows them to interpret these messages.

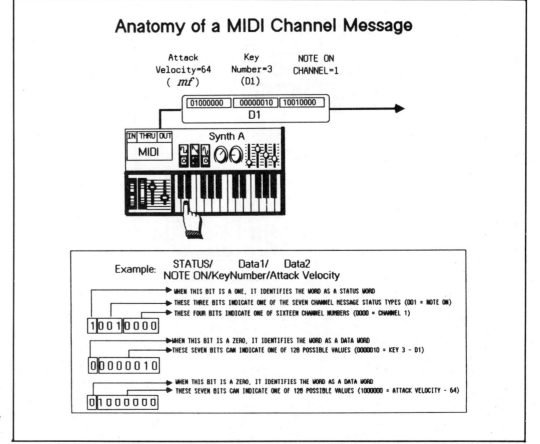

### Anatomy of a MIDI Channel Message

Attack Velocity=64 ( *mf* )  Key Number=3 (D1)  NOTE ON CHANNEL=1

`01000000` `00000010` `10010000`
D1

IN THRU OUT  MIDI  Synth A

Example: STATUS/ Data1/ Data2
NOTE ON/KeyNumber/Attack Velocity

`1 0 0 1 0 0 0 0`
- WHEN THIS BIT IS A ONE, IT IDENTIFIES THE WORD AS A STATUS WORD
- THESE THREE BITS INDICATE ONE OF THE SEVEN CHANNEL MESSAGE STATUS TYPES (001 = NOTE ON)
- THESE FOUR BITS INDICATE ONE OF SIXTEEN CHANNEL NUMBERS (0000 = CHANNEL 1)

`0 0 0 0 0 0 1 0`
- WHEN THIS BIT IS A ZERO, IT IDENTIFIES THE WORD AS A DATA WORD
- THESE SEVEN BITS CAN INDICATE ONE OF 128 POSSIBLE VALUES (0000010 = KEY 3 - D1)

`0 1 0 0 0 0 0 0`
- WHEN THIS BIT IS A ZERO, IT IDENTIFIES THE WORD AS A DATA WORD
- THESE SEVEN BITS CAN INDICATE ONE OF 128 POSSIBLE VALUES (1000000 = ATTACK VELOCITY - 64)

## 2.2.1 MIDI Channel Messages

MIDI channels are perhaps the most powerful aspect of the interface. Performance related messages can be assigned to one of sixteen different channels. Each channel can be an independent performance, played by a separate synthesizer or set of voices.

### MIDI Channel Voice Messages

| STATUS Word | Data Word 1 | Data Word 2 |
|---|---|---|
| **NOTE ON**<br>`1 0 0 1 ? ? ? ?`<br><br>INDICATES CHANNEL # 1-16<br><br>THIS MESSAGE IS ALSO USED TO INDICATE NOTE OFF BY TRANSMITTING IT WITH ATTACK VELOCITY DATA = 0. | **Key Number**<br>`0 ? ? ? ? ? ? ?`<br><br>INDICATES KEY # 0-127<br>60 = MIDDLE C | **Attack Velocity**<br>`0 ? ? ? ? ? ? ?`<br><br>INDICATES ATTACK VELOCITY 0-127<br>127=FFF<br>64=MF<br>(SENT BY NON-DYNAMIC KEYBOARDS)<br>0=NOTE OFF |
| **NOTE OFF**<br>`1 0 0 0 ? ? ? ?`<br><br>INDICATES CHANNEL # 1-16<br>THIS IS GENERALLY USED ONLY WITH INSTRUMENTS THAT CAN TRANSMIT RELEASE VELOCITY DATA | **Key Number**<br>`0 ? ? ? ? ? ? ?`<br><br>INDICATES KEY # 0-127<br>60 = MIDDLE C | **Release Velocity**<br>`0 ? ? ? ? ? ? ?`<br><br>INDICATES RELEASE VELOCITY 0-127<br>(IGNORED BY NON-DYNAMIC DEVICES) |
| **PITCH BENDER CHANGE**<br>`1 1 1 0 ? ? ? ?`<br><br>INDICATES CHANNEL # 1-16 | **Bender Position**<br>`0 ? ? ? ? ? ? ?`<br><br>127 = MAX SHARP<br>64 = CENTERED (NO CHANGE)<br>0 = MAX FLAT | **Bender Position 2**<br>`0 ? ? ? ? ? ? ?`<br><br>THIS OPTIONAL DATA CAN BE USED TO PROVIDE FINER RESOLUTION OF THE BENDER |
| **CONTROL CHANGE**<br>`1 0 1 1 ? ? ? ?`<br><br>INDICATES CHANNEL # 1-16 | **Controller Number**<br>`0 ? ? ? ? ? ? ?`<br><br>0-31 = CONTINUOUS CONTROLLER<br>64-95 = SWITCH CONTROLLER<br>122-127 = CHANNEL MODE MESSAGES | **Controller Position**<br>`0 ? ? ? ? ? ? ?`<br><br>127 = MAX OR ON<br>0 = MIN OR OFF |
| **POLYPHONIC KEY PRESSURE**<br>`1 0 1 0 ? ? ? ?`<br><br>INDICATES CHANNEL # 1-16 | **Key Number**<br>`0 ? ? ? ? ? ? ?`<br><br>INDICATES KEY # 0-127<br>60 = MIDDLE C | **After Touch**<br>`0 ? ? ? ? ? ? ?`<br><br>127 = MAX    0 = MIN<br>PRESSURE VALUE PER KEY |
| **CHANNEL PRESSURE**<br>`1 1 0 1 ? ? ? ?`<br><br>INDICATES CHANNEL # 1-16 | **After Touch**<br>`0 ? ? ? ? ? ? ?`<br><br>127 = MAX    0 = MIN<br>SAME VALUE FOR ALL NOTES | |
| **PROGRAM CHANGE**<br>`1 1 0 0 ? ? ? ?`<br><br>INDICATES CHANNEL # 1-16 | **Preset Number**<br>`0 ? ? ? ? ? ? ?`<br><br>INDICATES 1 OF 128 PRESETS | |

? = 1 bit (1 or 0)

4 bits can indicate any one of 16 values (0-15).

7 bits can indicate any one of 128 values (0-127).

### Channel Voice Messages

The majority of MIDI messages sent through the interface are *Channel Voice Messages*. These include all messages that originate as physical aspects of performance, including which keys are played, what foot switches or buttons are pushed, what continuous controllers (mod wheels, foot pedals, breath controllers, etc.) are moved, keyboard dynamics such as pressure and velocity sensitivity, and program change information as well.

Each instrument in a MIDI system can be assigned to a specific channel number (1-16). Once assigned to a specific channel, an instrument transmits and receives messages only on the assigned channel(s) and will ignore messages for other channels. **This makes it possible to route different performances to different instruments at the same time, over the same cable**. This is accomplished by assigning each instrument to a different MIDI channel.

### Examples of Channel Voice Messages

Here is a list of all of the Channel Voice Messages. The illustration shows more details about the actual commands and data they contain. **All parts of a message must be transmitted**. For example, the NOTE ON message must contain a Attack Velocity value even if the keyboard transmitting it is not velocity sensitive. In such an instance, the complete message would be transmitted with an Attack Velocity value of 64.

## NOTE ON/Key Number/Attack Velocity

This message is used to indicate that a key has been pushed down. There are two values that are always transmitted with this message. The *Key Number* is used to indicate one of 128 keys (1-127). Middle C is equal to Key Number 60. *Attack Velocity* is used to specify the rate of key depression on dynamic keyboards. It can have any value between 0 and 127. Velocity is most often used to control a sound's loudness. Since an Attack Velocity value must always be given in a NOTE ON message, nondynamic keyboards will transmit a value of 64 even though they are not capable of sensing velocity. **This ensures that a nondynamic keyboard can control a dynamic one** (see Section III: Applications). An Attack Velocity of zero (0) has a special meaning to MIDI instruments. All MIDI instruments will recognize NOTE ON/Key Number / Attack Velocity = 0 as a note OFF message. (See below for more about NOTE OFF.)

## NOTE OFF/Key Number/Release Velocity

Similar to NOTE ON, *NOTE OFF* messages are used to indicate which of 128 keys have been let up. If the keyboard can transmit the rate that a key is let up, the NOTE OFF message will contain a *Release Velocity* value between 0 and 127. If the keyboard isn't capable of transmitting Release Velocity data, it will probably transmit the Attack Velocity = 0 version of the NOTE ON message instead of this explicit NOTE OFF message. If a receiving instrument can't respond to Release Velocity data, it will act on the NOTE OFF/Key Number portions of the message and simply ignore the Release data. (This kind of information is detailed on an instrument's MIDI implementation chart.)

## PITCH BENDER CHANGE/Bender Position

This message is used to indicate that the pitch bender **has been moved**. It is sent whenever the position of the bender is changed. The *Bender Position* value indicates the current location of the bender as a number between 0 and 127. The value 64 is sent when the bender is moved to the centered (no pitch change) position. Manufacturers may choose to send an additional byte with this message to provide finer resolution for the bender. This additional data divides each of the 128 bender positions into finer detail. This optional data can split each step in up to 128 smaller steps. Sensitivity to the bender position is set at the receiving instrument.

## CONTROL CHANGE/Controller Number/Controller Position

This message can be used to indicate the movement of additional (optional) controllers. The *Controller Number* can indicate one of 64 potential controllers. The *Controller Position* value can indicate one of up to several thousand positions. However, the typical controller will transmit 128 positions. Controller Numbers 0-31 are used to identify continuous (knobs, sliders, wheels, etc.) controllers and 64-95 are used to identify switch (sustain pedals, buttons, etc.) controllers. See the Controller Number Chart for more details.

# MIDI Controller Numbers

## Continuous Controllers 0—63

| CONTROLLER NUMBER | | CONTROLLER NUMBER | |
|---|---|---|---|
| 0 | Continuous Controller 0 | 32 | Continuous Controller 0 |
| 1 | MOD Wheel | 33 | MOD Wheel |
| 2 | Continuous Controller 2 | 34 | Continuous Controller 2 |
| 3—31 | Continuous Controllers 3—31 | 35—63 | Continuous Controllers 3—31 |

Numbers 0—31 are used to indicate the 32 continuous controllers defined by MIDI. Note that #1 is reserved for the MOD wheel. The other numbers are not formally assigned to any particular controllers

Numbers 32—63 are used to transmit more position data for the 32 controllers. This is how high resclution data is transferred. Numbers 32—63 are not used to indicate additional controllers. Instead, they are used to transmit additional position data for 0—31.

## Switches 64—95

| CONTROLLER NUMBER | | CONTROLLER POSITION |
|---|---|---|
| 64 | Sustain Switch | 0 = OFF |
| 65—95 | Switch Controllers 65—95 | 127 = ON |

Numbers 64—95 are used to indicate the 32 possible MIDI switch controllers. Standard practice is to assign #64 to the SUSTAIN switch. The other switch numbers are not formally assigned to any particular switches.

Data word 2 of a CONTROL CHANGE message contains the position of the controller. In the case of switches, 0 indicates OFF and the value 127 indicates ON. For switches, values between 1 and 126 are ignored.

## Undefined Controller Numbers 96—121

The numbers 96 —121 are currently undefined. They are reserved for future use.

## Reserved For Channel Mode Messages 122—127

| | |
|---|---|
| 122 = LOCAL CONTROL ON/OFF | 125 = OMNI ON |
| 123 = ALL NOTES OFF | 126 = MONO ON (POLY OFF) |
| 124 = OMNI OFF | 127 = POLY ON (MONO OFF) |

The numbers 122 —127 have been set aside for use as Channel Mode Messages. They are not really CONTROL CHANGE messages, they share the same Status word. Except for LOCAL CONTROL ON/OFF, each of these messages may function as an ALL NOTES OFF message.

The Controller Number data of a CONTROL CHANGE message is used to specify 32 continuous controllers and 32 switches. Note that if high resolution continuous data is needed, a second CONTROL CHANGE message is sent with the additional data. Therefore, 64 numbers are reserved for use with 32 continuous controllers. Note also that numbers 122-127 specify Channel Mode Messages.

## POLYPHONIC KEY PRESSURE/Key Number/After Touch

This message is only transmitted by keyboards with **individual pressure sensitivity for each voice**. The *Key Number* value indicates which key is being pressed, and the *After Touch* value is used to specify a pressure amount (0-127).

## CHANNEL PRESSURE/After Touch

This message is transmitted by pressure-sensitive keyboards like the one found in the Yamaha DX7. **One pressure value is applied to all of the voices**. The message contains a single *After Touch* value (0-127).

## PROGRAM CHANGE/Preset Number

This message is used to change the current preset sound. The *Preset Number* value can indicate one of 128 possible presets.

## MIDI Channel Mode Messages

| STATUS Word | Data Word 1 | Data Word 2 |
|---|---|---|
| **CONTROL CHANGE**<br>`1 0 1 1 ? ? ? ?`<br>INDICATES CHANNEL # 1-16 | **LOCAL CONTROL**<br>`0 1 1 1 1 0 1 0`<br>122 = LOCAL CONTROL | **On/Off**<br>`0 ? ? ? ? ? ? ?`<br>127 = ON<br>0 = OFF |
| **CONTROL CHANGE**<br>`1 0 1 1 ? ? ? ?`<br>INDICATES CHANNEL # 1-16 | **ALL NOTES OFF**<br>`0 1 1 1 1 0 1 1`<br>123 = ALL NOTES OFF | **(no meaning)**<br>`0 0 0 0 0 0 0 0`<br>THIS DATA WORD MUST BE SENT BUT ITS VALUE IS IGNORED BY THE RECEIVING DEVICE |
| **CONTROL CHANGE**<br>`1 0 1 1 ? ? ? ?`<br>INDICATES CHANNEL # 1-16 | **OMNI ON**<br>`0 1 1 1 1 1 0 0`<br>124 = OMNI ON | **(no meaning)**<br>`0 0 0 0 0 0 0 0`<br>THIS DATA WORD MUST BE SENT BUT ITS VALUE IS IGNORED BY THE RECEIVING DEVICE |
| **CONTROL CHANGE**<br>`1 0 1 1 ? ? ? ?`<br>INDICATES CHANNEL # 1-16 | **OMNI OFF**<br>`0 1 1 1 1 1 0 1`<br>125 = OMNI OFF | **(no meaning)**<br>`0 0 0 0 0 0 0 0`<br>THIS DATA WORD MUST BE SENT BUT ITS VALUE IS IGNORED BY THE RECEIVING DEVICE |
| **CONTROL CHANGE**<br>`1 0 1 1 ? ? ? ?`<br>INDICATES CHANNEL # 1-16 | **MONO ON (POLY OFF)**<br>`0 1 1 1 1 1 1 0`<br>126 = MONO ON | **Channel Allocation**<br>`0 0 0 0 ? ? ? ?`<br>INDICATES THE NUMBER OF MONO CHANNELS TO ASSIGN VOICES TO |
| **CONTROL CHANGE**<br>`1 0 1 1 ? ? ? ?`<br>INDICATES CHANNEL # 1-16 | **POLY ON (MONO OFF)**<br>`0 1 1 1 1 1 1 1`<br>127 = POLY ON | **(no meaning)**<br>`0 0 0 0 0 0 0 0`<br>THIS DATA WORD MUST BE SENT BUT ITS VALUE IS IGNORED BY THE RECEIVING DEVICE |

Channel Mode Messages use the same format as the CONTROL CHANGE message. Therefore, each of these messages must contain two data words even though the second word is unnecessary for some of these messages. The OMNI On/Off and POLY/MONO messages also act as All Notes Off messages as well.

## MIDI Channel Mode Messages

In order to take most advantage of MIDI channels, several *MIDI modes* have been defined. This is an area of some confusion because, unfortunately, the terms used to describe the different modes (OMNI, POLY and MONO) have also been used (long before MIDI) to describe certain unrelated synthesizer functions or characteristics. The MIDI specification also allows the modes to be defined by numbers, i.e., Mode 1, 2, 3 or 4. It is not possible to know what to expect from a given mode by just a number alone; it is necessary to know what the numbers stand for. To make matters worse, some manufacturers use the terms OMNI, POLY and MONO incorrectly. **To accurately define a MINI mode, two terms must always be used together**, i.e., OMNI ON/POLY or OMNI OFF/MONO. Saying that an instrument is in the "OMNI mode" provides about as much information as saying that the instrument is turned on. No wonder there is confusion about MIDI modes!

Actually, it's quite simple and easy to understand. For the sake of consistency, we will describe the modes using the terminology set forth in the formal definitions of the MIDI specification.

There are two factors to be aware of in each MIDI mode: *channel assignment* (OMNI ON or OMNI OFF) and *voice assignment* (POLY or MONO). Channel assignment allows you to decide which MIDI channel(s) a particular instrument will respond to. Voice assignment allows you to decide if an instrument's voices will be assigned to channels polyphonically (more than one voice per channel) or monophonically (one voice per channel). **It is important to realize that this ability to split voices is not available on every synthesizer**. It is a special feature that may or may not be included in an instrument's MIDI design.

## Channel Assignment

### OMNI ON

When set to *OMNI ON*, an instrument will try to respond to all messages it receives (via MIDI IN) regardless of their channel assignments. All messages the instrument transmits (via MIDI OUT) will be assigned to one channel. If an instrument is not capable of channel assignment (see OMNI OFF), this must be channel 1. Otherwise, this can be any of the sixteen MIDI channels. Common practice, however, is always to use channel 1.

### OMNI OFF

When set to OMNI OFF, the instrument can be assigned to a specific MIDI channel. It will only try to respond to messages on the assigned channel(s) and will ignore messages on any other channel. The instrument will transmit voice messages only on the assigned channel(s). It is common practice to assign both the receive and transmit channels to the same number. However, some instruments can transmit and receive on different channels.

The display associated with this function will generally show "OMNI" or "ALL" when set to OMNI ON, and a channel number, which can be changed from 1 to 16, when set to OMNI OFF.

### Voice Assignment

Most synthesizers assign their internal voices to a single preset. All of the notes have the same sound. Some instruments allow the voice assignment to be "split" between two or more presets at a time. For example, voices might be split between the left and right side of the keyboard, each side having its own sound. Some instruments can split **each voice** to a **different preset**.

MIDI allows an instrument to assign voices to channels **polyphonically** (more than one note per channel) or **monophonically** (only one note per channel). MIDI can take advantage of these two modes of voice assignment only if the instrument incorporates them in its MIDI design.

### POLY

When a synthesizer assigns its voices to presets polyphonically, it is in a *POLY mode*. Most synthesizers can only assign their voices to one preset at a time. Some can split voices into groups, making it possible to split the keyboard or layer sounds. In such situations, the instrument behaves as though it were two (or more) individual polyphonic synthesizers.

### MONO

If an instrument can assign each of its voices to a different preset, it is said to be in a *MONO mode*. For example, a six-voice instrument set to the MONO mode would behave like six individual monophonic synthesizers. This sophisticated voice assignment is not common on most synthesizers.

## The Four MIDI Modes

The combinations of OMNI ON/OMNI OFF and POLY/MONO yield four MIDI modes. An instrument will always be in one of the four modes at any given time.

### OMNI ON/POLY (MIDI MODE 1)

This is the standard MIDI mode. When an instrument is first turned on, it should automatically set itself to this mode. In this mode a synth will try to respond to any channel messages arriving at its MIDI IN port, regardless of channel information. All voices will be assigned to one preset sound.

When in the *OMNI ON/POLY mode*, an instrument will transmit voice messages, via MIDI OUT, on a single channel. If this is the only mode the instrument supports, then this must be channel 1. Otherwise, it can be any channel. Common practice, however, is to use channel 1 for transmission in the OMNI ON/POLY mode.

## MIDI Mode 1: OMNI ON/POLY

Messages from external MIDI source

| C1 CHANNEL1 | G1 CHANNEL 2 | E2 CHANNEL 1 | A2 CHANNEL 3 | D3 CHANNEL 1 | F#3 CHANNEL 2 |

IN   THRU   OUT

All voices play the same preset sound

Voice 1  Voice 2  Voice 3  Voice 4  Voice 5  Voice 6

(Microprocessor)   C1
G1
OMNI ON/POLY   E2
(Ignore channel info)   A2
D3
F#3

BEND MOD RATE RANGE

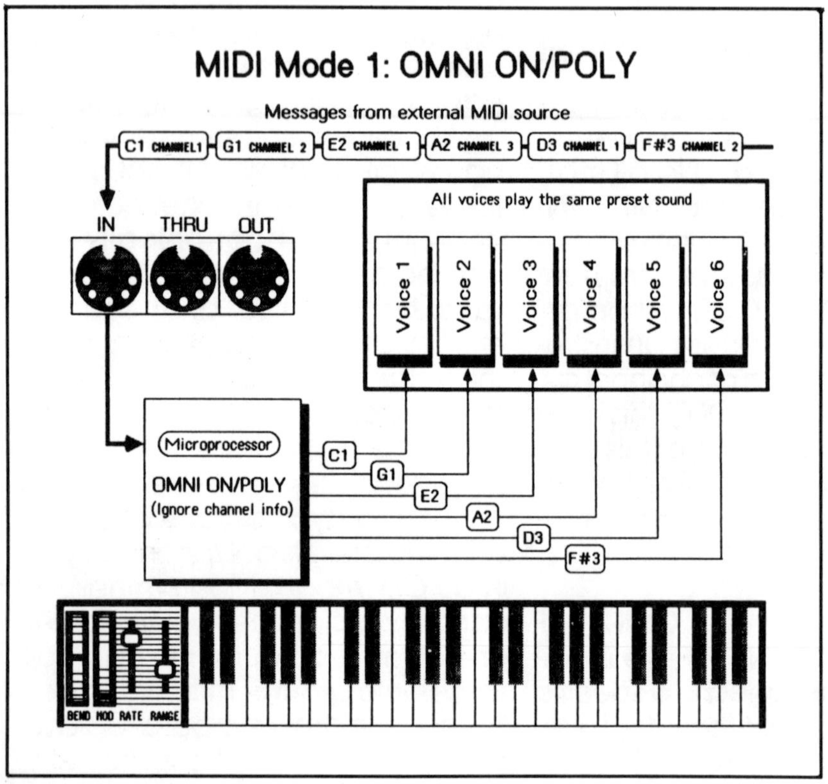

In this MIDI mode, an instrument will respond to ALL Channel Voice Messages, regardless of their individual channel assignments. All of the instrument's internal voices will be assigned to the same preset sound. MIDI messages sent from an instrument in this mode will all be assigned to a single channel. If this is the only mode the instrument supports, then that channel must be channel 1.

In the OMNI OFF/POLY mode, you can select what channel(s) an instrument will respond to. In this example, the synth has been set to receive messages on MIDI channel 2. It only plays notes that are assigned to channel 2 and ignores messages assigned to any other channel. MIDI messages sent from this instrument will all be assigned to the selected channel.

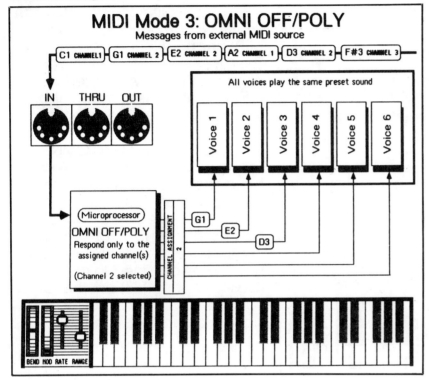

## MIDI Mode 3: OMNI OFF/POLY
### Messages from external MIDI source

## MIDI Mode 3: Variation (Dual Channel Assignment)
### Messages from external MIDI source

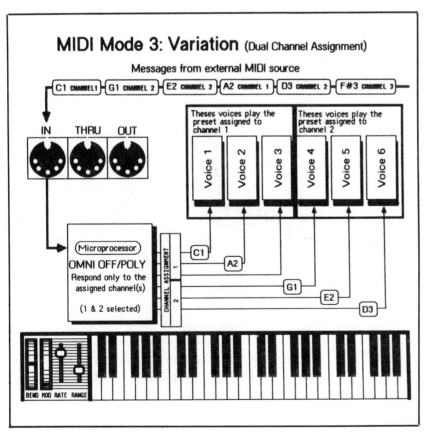

## OMNI OFF / POLY (MIDI MODE 3)

This mode allows you to select which channel(s) the synthesizer will respond to. If, for example, the instrument was set to channel 2, then it would only play those meassages that have been assigned to channel 2 (while ignoring all messages on other channels). In most cases, all voices will be assigned to one preset sound.

All voice messages transmitted by the insrument would be assigned to one channel. Typically, this is the same channel as the receive channel(in this case, 2). It is possible, however, to select different transmit and receive channels on some instruments.

If the instrument can assign its voices to different presets polyphonically (via keyboard splits or layers), then each group of voices can be assigned a separate MIDI channel. This feature, not available on all synthesizers, turns an instrument into two or more independent polyphonic synthesizers.

The selected channel is called the *base channel*. If the instrument can be split into two groups of voices, then it will respond to two channels: the base channel and the next higher channel number. On some instruments, the two keyboard sections can be assigned to any MIDI channels. They are not limited to the base channel and base channel +1 method of assignment.

Some instruments can assign groups of voices to different preset sounds. In such a case, it may be possible to assign each group of voices to different MIDI channels. This optional feature essentially turns one instrument into two polyphonic synthesizers.

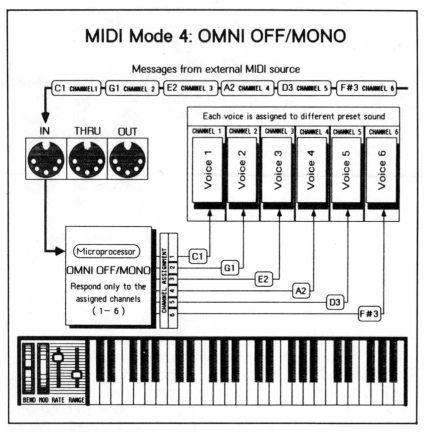

MIDI Mode 4: OMNI OFF/MONO

Messages from external MIDI source

C1 CHANNEL1 — G1 CHANNEL 2 — E2 CHANNEL 3 — A2 CHANNEL 4 — D3 CHANNEL 5 — F#3 CHANNEL 6

IN    THRU    OUT

Each voice is assigned to different preset sound

CHANNEL 1  CHANNEL 2  CHANNEL 3  CHANNEL 4  CHANNEL 5  CHANNEL 6

Voice 1  Voice 2  Voice 3  Voice 4  Voice 5  Voice 6

Microprocessor

OMNI OFF/MONO

Respond only to the assigned channels (1–6)

CHANNEL ASSIGNMENT

C1  G1  E2  A2  D3  F#3

BEND  MOD  RATE  RANGE

The OMNI OFF/MONO mode can only be used by instruments that can assign each voice to a different preset. Each voice will respond to a different MIDI channel, one channel per voice. In this mode, a six-voice polyphonic synthesizer would behave like six monophonic synthesizers.

## OMNI OFF/MONO (MIDI Mode 4)

This mode can only be utilized by instruments that can assign each voice to a different preset. **Each voice will respond to a different MIDI channel**, one for each voice. This turns the synthesizer into a group of monophonic synthesizers.

Each of these monophonic voices is assigned a different channel number, starting with the one you select when setting OMNI OFF. The selected channel is called the base channel. If the instrument has six voices, then it will respond to six channels: the selected base channel and the next five higher channel numbers. For example, if the instrument were assigned to channel 3 (base channel), then the other voices would automatically be assigned to channels 4 through 8.

## OMNI ON/MONO (MIDI Mode 2)

This is not a particularly useful MIDI mode, and is included here only for the sake of completeness. In this mode, all voice channel messages received will be assigned to a single voice monophonically (regardless of their channel assignments).

When transmitting in this mode, messages for only one voice are sent via one channel.

This mode is intended to be used when interfacing monophonic instruments with polyphonic ones. It is not needed when interfacing polyphonic instruments together.

## Examples of MIDI Channel Mode Messages

Channel Mode Messages are special versions of the CONTROL CHANGE message. Each of these messages is three words long. The first word (status word) is the same word used to indicate a CONTROL CHANGE. The value of the second word in the message identifies it as a Channel Mode Message. The values 122 through 127 have been reserved for this purpose, making it possible to define 6 different Channel Mode Messages. **Because of this, these numbers cannot be used to define MIDI controllers.** (Valid MIDI controller numbers are 0-31 and 64-96.)

### CONTROL CHANGE/ LOCAL CONTROL/On-Off

This message is used to **disconnect** an instrument's keyboard from its internal voices. The voices can then be controlled via the MIDI IN port. Following the CONTROL CHANGE status word, a value of 122 in data word 2 identifies this as a LOCAL CONTROL message. The value of data word 3 indicates whether LOCAL CONTROL is OFF (value = 0) or ON (value = 127).

### CONTROL CHANGE/ ALL NOTES OFF/0

This message causes any receiving instruments on the same channel as the one contained in the CONTROL CHANGE status word to turn off all voices that are on when the message is received. A value of 123 in data word 2 indicates that this is an ALL NOTES OFF message. The value of data word 3 is not used, but since this is a CONTROL CHANGE message, **it must be three words long.** This third word is given a value of 0. Not all MIDI instruments recognize this message.

### CONTROL CHANGE/ OMNI ON-OFF/0

This message is used to transmit the OMNI aspect of the MIDI modes. OMNI OFF is indicated with a value of 124, and OMNI ON is indicated with a value of 125. The value of the third word is not used but must be transmitted since the message must be three words long.

### CONTROL CHANGE/ MONO-POLY/Mono Channels

This message is used to tell a receiving instrument to switch to either the MONO or POLY mode. A value of 126 indicates MONO and 127 is used to indicate POLY. The value of the third word is used to indicate how many mono channels the receiving instrument should allocate to its internal voices. The four mode related messages, Ommi On, Ommi Off, Poly On, and Mono On also function as all notes off messages as well.

Unlike channel messages, which can be sent to specific devices within a MIDI system, system messages will be **received by all instruments interfaced via MIDI**. These messages are used to communicate information useful to the MIDI system as a whole. System messages contain no channel information and are available to any instrument (regardless of its MIDI mode or channel assignment) that can make use of them. Below is a list of the most commonly used MIDI System Messages.

## System Common Messages

**These messages are intended for use with master controllers, drum machines and sequencers**. Not all equipment makes use of these messages at this time, but it is an indication of the flexibility and expansion built in to MIDI.

### SONG POSITION/Pointer Number1
### Pointer Number 2

This message can indicate a location within a MIDI sequence (sequencer or drum patterns). The Pointer Number value contains the number of sixteenth notes since the start of the sequence.

### SONG SELECT/Song Number

This message is sent to select a specific preset MIDI song from a drum machine or sequencer. It does not contain any performance information, only the Song Number value (0-127) indicating the number of a preset song.

### TUNE REQUEST

When an instrument receives this message, it will perform its tuning routine (if it has one). Tune Request does not transmit any kind of tuning standard such as A-440. It does not ensure that individual instruments will be in tune with each other.

### MIDI System Common Messages

| STATUS Word | Data Word 1 | Data Word 2 |
|---|---|---|
| SONG POSITION  `1 1 1 1 0 0 1 0` | Pointer Number (1)  `0 ? ? ? ? ? ? ?`  THESE TWO BYTES ARE USED TO INDICTATE A LOCATION WITHIN A MIDI SONG | Pointer Number (2)  `0 ? ? ? ? ? ? ?`  THE LOCATION IS GIVEN AS ONE OF 16,384 16TH NOTES (0 IS THE FIRST NOTE OF THE SONG) |
| SONG SELECT  `1 1 1 1 0 0 1 1` | Song Number  `0 ? ? ? ? ? ? ?`  INDICATES 1 OF 128 SONGS | |
| TUNE REQUEST  `1 1 1 1 0 1 1 0` | | |

System Common Messages are available to all devices in a MIDI system regardless of their channel or mode assignments. Note that there is no need to carry channel information within the status words of these messages.

## MIDI System Real Time Messages

### STATUS Word

**MIDI CLOCK**

| 1 | 1 | 1 | 1 | 1 | 0 | 0 | 0 |
|---|---|---|---|---|---|---|---|

**START**

| 1 | 1 | 1 | 1 | 1 | 0 | 1 | 0 |
|---|---|---|---|---|---|---|---|

**CONTINUE**

| 1 | 1 | 1 | 1 | 1 | 0 | 1 | 1 |
|---|---|---|---|---|---|---|---|

**STOP**

| 1 | 1 | 1 | 1 | 1 | 1 | 0 | 0 |
|---|---|---|---|---|---|---|---|

**ACTIVE SENSING**

| 1 | 1 | 1 | 1 | 1 | 1 | 1 | 0 |
|---|---|---|---|---|---|---|---|

**SYSTEM RESET**

| 1 | 1 | 1 | 1 | 1 | 1 | 1 | 1 |
|---|---|---|---|---|---|---|---|

Like System Common Messages, System Real Time Messages are available to all instruments in a MIDI system, regardless of channel or mode assignments. Note that there are no data words associated with Real Time Messages. Each message consists of a single status word.

## System Real Time Messages

These messages have to do with the timing-reference aspect of the MIDI interface.

### MIDI CLOCK

The MIDI Clock is transmitted over the same cable as all of the other MIDI messages. It divides a beat into 24 subdivisions, giving a resolution to 64th-note triplets. The MIDI clock is only used by sequencers, arpeggiators and drum machines as a **timing reference**.

The MIDI clock is transmitted as a binary code. It is not electronically compatible with other 24-beat-subdivision clocks (see Section III).

### START

This message is sent when the "PLAY" button is hit on a master controller. It will start any connected MIDI sequencers and drum machines at the beginning of their sequence.

### STOP

This message is sent when the "STOP" button is pressed on a master controller, stopping all MIDI sequencers and drum machines.

### CONTINUE

When the "CONTINUE" button is hit, all MIDI drum machines and sequencers will begin again from where they left off when the STOP message was received.

### ACTIVE SENSING

The MIDI spec. defines an ACTIVE SENSING mode. When operating in this mode, the transmitter will periodically send this message whenever it is idle. The purpose of this message is to allow receiving instruments to verify that the MIDI connections between them and the transmitter are OK. (In other words, no one has accidently unplugged a cable!) When an instrument that uses ACTIVE SENSING receives this message, it will look for further MIDI activity at its IN port. If no new MIDI messages (or another ACTIVE SENSING message) arrive within 300 ms, the receiver will assume its connection with the transmitting instrument has been disrupted in some way. It will shut off any currently sounding notes and return to normal operation. Although this system was used on some early instruments, as this book goes to press, very few newer instruments make use of this ACTIVE SENSING. It is included here mainly for the sake of completeness.

### SYSTEM RESET

When this message is received, an instrument will return to the **default** settings it uses when first powered up. Not all MIDI instruments will recognize this message.

## System Exclusive Messages

System Exclusive Messages allow MIDI devices to transmit information that has meaning only to certain instruments, without "confusing" other MIDI instruments in the system. For instance, it might be convenient to send parameter settings between two synths of the same make and model (like two DX7s). That information would be meaningless to a Super Jupiter, or Casio CZ5000 also connected to the same system.

System Exclusive Messages are used to send/receive device dependent messages through the MIDI interface without "confusing" instruments which they are not intended for. This system is used to transfer such instrument-unique information as sound data, sample dumps, sequence dumps, and voicing parameters.

### SYSTEM EXCLUSIVE / MANUFACTURER ID

The first word in an Exclusive Message is an ID number. Each manufacturer has a different one. This is what tells an instrument whether it should **ignore** or **respond** to the rest of the message.

### Exclusive Messages

Immediately following the ID is whatever information belongs to the message. This can be anything. Typical messages are program dumps, sequence dumps, sampling data, and voicing parameters. These are the messages that are used by the various voicing programs available for personal computers.

### EOX (End Of Exclusive Message)

The last word of an Exclusive Message is a code that indicates the message is over. This tells other instruments to **stop ignoring messages**.

| MIDI System Exclusive Messages | | |
|---|---|---|
| STATUS Word | Data Word 1 | Additional Data |
| SYSTEM EXCLUSIVE<br>`1 1 1 1 0 0 0 0` | Manufacturer ID<br>`0 ? ? ? ? ? ? ?`<br>THIS WORD IS USED TO INDICATE THE SPECIFIC MANUFACTURER THE MESSAGE IS MEANT FOR | `0 ? ? ? ? ? ? ?`<br>ANY NUMBER OF ADDITIONAL DATA WORDS CAN FOLLOW THE ID. THESE WILL DEFINE THE ACTUAL MESSAGE. |
| END OF EXCLUSIVE<br>`1 1 1 1 0 1 1 1` | | |

If a device does not recognize the Manufacturer ID number that follows the System Exclusive status word, it simply ignores the rest of the Exclusive message.

Since the message can be of any length, the END OF EXCLUSIVE message is used to signal that an Exclusive message is completed. This also signals the other devices in the system to start paying attention to MIDI messages again.

## 2.3.0 MIDI IN THE REAL WORLD

Since there are so many different kinds of synthesizers, with so many kinds of different features and functions, how does MIDI deal with the incongruities that must inevitably arise when various instruments are interfaced together? Not all MIDI instruments will have the same features, such as the same number of voices, dynamic keyboards, or the same number of presets, etc.

What happens when a non velocity-sensitive instrument receives velocity data as part of a NOTE ON message? Or an instrument with 32 presets receives a message to change to preset #65? Have no fear. **Messages that have no meaning to an individual instrument are simply ignored.** Since velocity data has no meaning to a non-dynamic instrument, the NOTE ON part of the message is acted upon and the velocity data is ignored. In the case of the presets, since the instrument doesn't have a preset numbered 65, the instrument ignores the message and continues playing the current preset.

If you use an eight-voice synth to control a six-voice synth and play an eight-note chord, will the six-voice instrument play eight notes? No. The six-voice will behave exactly as though you played eight keys on its keyboard and ignore two of the notes you're holding down.

## 2.3.1 Evaluating Factory Implementations of MIDI

**Not all instruments utilize every MIDI feature.** Most use a meaningful subset of all of the possible MIDI functions. It is necessary to understand which MIDI functions a particular instrument does or doesn't have, in order to get the most from both the instrument and the interface.

### The Minimum Implementation

As well as the MIDI interface is defined, there is no definition as to which MIDI features must be included in an instrument in order for it to be considered MIDI. This means that you can't take anything for granted. In the case of a typical polyphonic synthesizer, you can almost always assume at least this much when you turn it on:

1. The instrument is in the OMNI ON/POLY mode. It will transmit on one channel (probably channel 1) and receive on all channels.

2. It will transmit and receive NOTE ON and NOTE OFF messages. (It might not transmit the dynamic Velocity data associated with these messages.)

### Optional MIDI Features

**Anything beyond these basic functions is an option.** Since there are so many different instruments, we can't list each one's implementation here. The only way to know what options an instrument supports is to read its manual. We can, however, give you a list of the possibilities.

### Optional Channel Mode Messages

The different MIDI modes offer a great deal of flexibility and freedom in setting up a MIDI system. **Not every synthesizer can utilize every mode.** If an instrument can only play one preset at a time, then it will always be in one of the two POLY modes. If the instrument can split its keyboard or layer sounds polyphonically, it might be able to assign separate channels to each split or layer. If it is multi-timbral (each voice can be assigned to a different preset), then it might be able to function in the MONO modes. The owner's manual will describe which modes that the insrument can support, as well as what channel(s) it is assigned to when the power is first turned on.

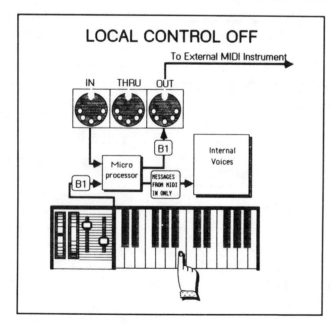

### OMNI OFF/POLY

This allows the instrument to be assigned to receive and transmit on any one of sixteen MIDI channels. Usually the same channel is used for both functions. However, some instruments can be assigned to receive and transmit on different channels.

If the instrument can assign groups of voices to different presets polyphonically, then each group can be assigned a separate MIDI channel. Each group of voices will act like an independent polyphonic instrument.

### OMNI OFF/MONO

This mode will only be found on instruments that can assign each internal voice to a different preset. Each voice will be assigned to receive/transmit on a separate MIDI channel. The synthesizer will behave like a set of independent monophonic instruments.

### LOCAL CONTROL OFF

This option allows you to **disconnect the instrument's keyboard from its internal voices**. Channel Voice Messages generated by playing on the keyboard are sent only to the MIDI OUT jack. If the instrument has an onboard sequencer for instance, this could make it possible for the sequencer to play the internal voices, while the keyboard is used to play an external slave instrument (via MIDI OUT), but not its own internal voices.

## Optional Channel Voice Messages

**All voice messages other than NOTE ON and NOTE OFF are optional**. Even though a MIDI instrument may have a particular synthesizer feature like pitch bend, it does not necessarily mean that the instrument is capable of transmitting or receiving MIDI pitch bend messages. We repeat, the only way to know for sure is to read each instrument's manual.

### MIDI Dynamics: Velocity

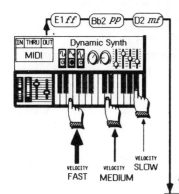

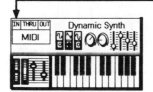

VELOCITY FAST   VELOCITY MEDIUM   VELOCITY SLOW

In this example, performance messages containing Velocity data are sent to two different synthesizers (using the daisy chain configuration).

Both instruments receive exactly the same messages. However, they each respond differently.

The non-dynamic instrument can not respond to the Velocity data in the messages, so it simply ignores it. The synth plays the note the only way it can; each one has the same loudness.

The dynamic instrument can respond to velocity data. It plays each note with the same relative dynamics that the performer played. Note that even though the non-dynamic synth couldn't respond to the Velocity data, that information was still sent through the THRU port to the other synth.

## ENABLE/DISABLE

Not all instruments respond the same way to certain Channel Voice Messages. For example, the range of the pitch bender might be permanently set for a minor third on one synth and a whole step on another. One unit might have its presets numbered consecutively from 1 to 64 and another might have four banks numbered A0 to D9. For this reason, many of these optional voice messages can be enabled or disabled so an instrument can be set to either **transmit, receive or ignore** these various options. Check the manual to find out which messages (if any) can be selectively turned on or off. Here is a list of the optional Channel Voice Messages:

### Attack/Release Velocities

MIDI Attack Velocity can have a value from 1 to 127. Nondynamic MIDI keyboards will always transmit an Attack Velocity value of 64 as part of the NOTE ON message, and ignore any received velocity values. This ensures that a nondynamic keyboard can play, or be played by, a dynamic keyboard.

Most dynamic keyboards, at this time, only transmit Attack Velocity, but more and more are adding Release Velocity as well. Some nondynamic keyboards, although incapable of transmitting dynamic velocity data, can respond to dynamic velocity data received via MIDI IN.

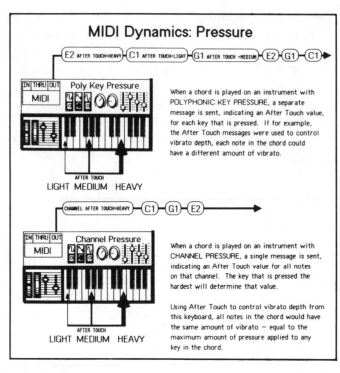

### MIDI Dynamics: Pressure

E2 AFTER TOUCH=HEAVY — C1 AFTER TOUCH=LIGHT — G1 AFTER TOUCH =MEDIUM — E2 — G1 — C1 ►

**Poly Key Pressure**
IN THRU OUT
MIDI

When a chord is played on an instrument with POLYPHONIC KEY PRESSURE, a separate message is sent, indicating an After Touch value, for each key that is pressed. If for example, the After Touch messages were used to control vibrato depth, each note in the chord could have a different amount of vibrato.

AFTER TOUCH
LIGHT MEDIUM HEAVY

CHANNEL AFTER TOUCH=HEAVY — C1 — G1 — E2 ►

**Channel Pressure**
IN THRU OUT
MIDI

When a chord is played on an instrument with CHANNEL PRESSURE, a single message is sent, indicating an After Touch value for all notes on that channel. The key that is pressed the hardest will determine that value.

Using After Touch to control vibrato depth from this keyboard, all notes in the chord would have the same amount of vibrato — equal to the maximum amount of pressure applied to any key in the chord.

AFTER TOUCH
LIGHT MEDIUM HEAVY

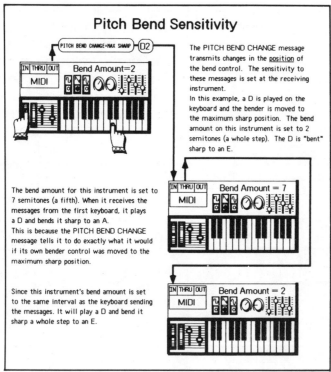

### Pitch Bend Sensitivity

PITCH BEND CHANGE=MAX SHARP — D2

**Bend Amount=2**
IN THRU OUT
MIDI

The PITCH BEND CHANGE message transmits changes in the <u>position</u> of the bend control. The sensitivity to these messages is set at the receiving instrument.
In this example, a D is played on the keyboard and the bender is moved to the maximum sharp position. The bend amount on this instrument is set to 2 semitones (a whole step). The D is "bent" sharp to an E.

The bend amount for this instrument is set to 7 semitones (a fifth). When it receives the messages from the first keyboard, it plays a D and bends it sharp to an A.
This is because the PITCH BEND CHANGE message tells it to do exactly what it would if its own bender control was moved to the maximum sharp position.

**Bend Amount = 7**
IN THRU OUT
MIDI

Since this instrument's bend amount is set to the same interval as the keyboard sending the messages. It will play a D and bend it sharp a whole step to an E.

**Bend Amount = 2**
IN THRU OUT
MIDI

### POLYPHONIC KEY PRESSURE

An instrument with independent pressure sensitivity for each voice could transmit this message. (Yamaha DX1, Kurzweil MIDI Board)

### CHANNEL PRESSSURE

This is the standard type of pressure sensitivity. A single value applies to all notes in a given channel. (Yamaha DX7, Fender Polaris)

### PITCH BEND CHANGE

**Any change in the position** of the synthesizer's pitch bender is transmitted with this message. Since it is the position that is transmitted, the amount of bend may be different between two instruments.

Moving a bender all the way up on synth-A might bend a note sharp by a whole step, while on synth-B all the way might cause a bend of a fifth. The amount of bend can be made compatible if at least one of the instruments has an adjustable pitch bend range (see Section III: Applications).

## CONTROL CHANGE

MIDI can also transmit the position of up to 32 additional continuous controllers (wheels, sliders, levers, pedals, etc.), as well as up to 32 on/off switches (buttons, foot switches, etc.). They are numbered 0-31 and 64-95 respectively. **A MIDI instrument must recognize the** controller's number or it will not respond to the changes even if they are being transmitted.

The only controllers formally defined by MIDI are the pitch bender and mod wheel. Below is a chart showing some commonly used controller assignments. (In the future some of these assignments will probably be permanently assigned.) MIDI manufacturers may assign undefined controllers to any valid MIDI controller number at their discretion. There is no guarantee that two instruments will use the same controller number for the same type of control device. For example, one instrument may assign its foot pedal to number 4, while another might assign its pedal to number 7. In such a case neither instrument would recognize changes of position of the other's foot pedal.

The best way to ensure that these optional MIDI continuous controllers and switches are recognized by all devices in a system is to make their identification numbers user assignable. Unfortunately, this kind of flexibility is not common. The owner's manual will tell you what numbers an instrument's controllers are (or can be) assigned to.

### Commonly Used MIDI Controller Assignments

| CONTINUOUS CONTROLLERS | | SWITCH CONTROLLERS | |
|---|---|---|---|
| 1 | Modulation Wheel | 64 | Sustain Switch |
| 2 | Breath Controller | 65 | Portamento Switch |
| 4 | Foot Control | 66 | Sustenuto Switch |
| 5 | Portamento Time | 67 | Soft Switch |
| 6 | Data Entry | | |
| 7 | Master Volume | | |

### Comparison of Preset Numbers

| SYNTH A | SYNTH B | SYNTH C | SYNTH A | SYNTH B | SYNTH C | SYNTH A | SYNTH B | SYNTH C | SYNTH A | SYNTH B | SYNTH C |
|---|---|---|---|---|---|---|---|---|---|---|---|
| 1 | 11 | A1 | 9 | 21 | A9 | 17 | 31 | B1 | 25 | 41 | B9 |
| 2 | 12 | A2 | 10 | 22 | A10 | 18 | 32 | B2 | 26 | 42 | B10 |
| 3 | 13 | A3 | 11 | 23 | A11 | 19 | 33 | B3 | 27 | 43 | B11 |
| 4 | 14 | A4 | 12 | 24 | A12 | 20 | 34 | B4 | 28 | 44 | B12 |
| 5 | 15 | A5 | 13 | 25 | A13 | 21 | 35 | B5 | 29 | 45 | B13 |
| 6 | 16 | A6 | 14 | 26 | A14 | 22 | 36 | B6 | 30 | 46 | B14 |
| 7 | 17 | A7 | 15 | 27 | A15 | 23 | 37 | B7 | 31 | 47 | B15 |
| 8 | 18 | A8 | 16 | 28 | A16 | 24 | 38 | B8 | 32 | 48 | B16 |

The MIDI PROGRAM CHANGE messages transmit numbers 0-127 to indicate a total of 128 possible presets. However, not all instruments number their presets from 0 to 127. This chart shows how three different synths, each with a different numbering system, would respond to the same PROGRAM CHANGE messages.

Each synth has 32 presets, but they use different methods of labeling. On Synth A they are numbered 1-32. Synth B has 4 banks (1-4). Each bank has 8 presets (1-8). Synth C has two banks (A and B). Each bank has sixteen presets (1-16).

The chart above shows the equivalent preset numbers for the three instruments. If Synth A was sending PROGRAM CHANGE messages to the other two synths; and preset number 1 was selected, then Synths B and C would change to presets 11 and A1 respectively. If Synth A were changed to preset 23, then the other two would change to 37 and B7 and so on.

## PROGRAM CHANGE

This message can select one of 128 preset program numbers. It is important to realize that programming parameters are not sent by this message. It is only used to indicate which particular **preset numbers** an instrument should switch to.

If this number is greater than the total number of presets an instrument has, it will be ignored. The chart below shows how programs will change when instruments with dissimilar preset numbering systems are used.

## 2.4.0 THERE ARE LIMITS

Think for a minute about all of the different messages that can be sent through a MIDI system. The implications are staggering to say the least. Theoretically, MIDI can transmit **sixteen** independent musical performances, each with up to **128 notes of polyphony**. Every one of these notes could have independent **Attack and Release Velocities**, as well as **After Touch**. Each of the channels could have independent **pitch bend** and effects controlled by **64 different** controllers.

This sounds like the answer to every musician's prayers, but there's a catch: MIDI is a *serial interface*. Remember the train station? Each message arrives or leaves **one bit at a time**. The messages travel at a fixed rate 31,250 bits a second. That seems pretty fast, but remember that a MIDI message is made up of several eight-bit words. A short musical phrase might be made up of hundreds of messages. Each message takes time to travel through the interface. It is possible for those messages to pile up, causing delays and errors.

## 2.4.1 Too Much of a Good Thing

There are limits to the number of messages that can be sent via MIDI before delays become unacceptable. The **limits are determined by** the length of the messages, the transmission rate of the interface, and the rate at which they are transferred to and from the interface by the microprocessor.

When two instruments are interfaced with MIDI, there are three significant delays that occur between the time a key is pressed on the first synthesizer, and the time the second synthesizer plays the note.

When the key is pressed, it takes between five and seven milliseconds (thousandths of a second) for the processor to **transfer the message** to the MIDI OUT port. This is the

same amount of time it takes for the instrument to play the note with its internal voices.

The NOTE ON message (three eight-bit words) takes less than one millisecond to travel between instruments via MIDI.

It takes another five to seven milliseconds for the processor of synthesizer #2 to transfer the message to its own internal hardware. It plays its note between six to eight milliseconds after synth #1, and between eleven to fifteen milliseconds after the key was originally pushed down.

How long is one millisecond? The time between 64th notes at a tempo of 120 beats per minute is about 60 milliseconds. The delay time between the two instruments in the

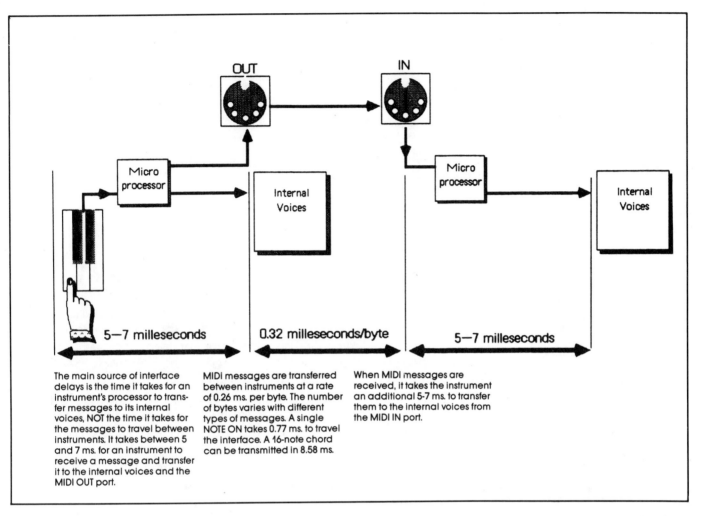

OUT

IN

Micro processor

Internal Voices

Micro processor

Internal Voices

5—7 milleseconds

0.32 milleseconds/byte

5—7 milleseconds

The main source of interface delays is the time it takes for an instrument's processor to transfer messages to its internal voices, NOT the time it takes for the messages to travel between instruments. It takes between 5 and 7 ms. for an instrument to receive a message and transfer it to the internal voices and the MIDI OUT port.

MIDI messages are transferred between instruments at a rate of 0.26 ms. per byte. The number of bytes varies with different types of messages. A single NOTE ON takes 0.77 ms. to travel the interface. A 16-note chord can be transmitted in 8.58 ms.

When MIDI messages are received, it takes the instrument an additional 5-7 ms. to transfer them to the internal voices from the MIDI IN port.

above example is less then the duration of one beat of a 256th-note triplet at the same tempo.

Much has been written about MIDI being "too slow" to be an effective interface. This is not really true. In terms of performance events, the MIDI transmission rate of 31.25 KBaud is quite fast. **MIDI can transmit over one thousand NOTE ON or NOTE OFF messages per second**! Notes occuring at that rate would be imperceptible as individual events. (We would hear a pitch more than two octaves above "A-440" instead!) Musical performances consist of more than just NOTE ON and NOTE OFF messages. Keep in mind that **After Touch, Pitch Bend, etc., are messages**

**too**. Even so, when playing single-note melodies, the main source of delays associated with MIDI interfacing is not the rate that MIDI transfers its messages between instruments. Most delays are incurred by the time taken by an instrument's processor to act on and transfer messages to and from the MIDI ports.

In any case, there is a point where delays will become noticeable. This point is directly related to the **number of notes** being played at once and how **quickly they are played**. It is not possible to say how many notes can be played at once before delays become unacceptable. The messages needed to convey a ten-note chord can be transmitted through the MIDI interface in 6.7 milliseconds, a sixteen-note chord in 10.56 milliseconds, and a thirty-two-note chord in 20.8 milliseconds. When the polyphony is ten notes or less, most of the overall delay is caused by an instrument's operating software, not the MIDI interface.

Don't despair. Most people won't bump up against this theoretical limit. It is safe to assume that an in-dividual performer cannot outplay the MIDI interface. When several performances are occuring at the same time, as is the case with a multi-track sequencer controlling several independent polyphonic instruments, unacceptable delays can occur. There are simple solutions to this kind of problem (see Section III).

### 2.4.2 The THRU Box

Another common MIDI problem is associated with the use of THRU ports. Each time you connect two units together via this port, the digital signal is degraded slightly. This small amount of distortion is not a problem because digital systems are fairly tolerant of distortion (another advantage of using digital signals to convey information). However, if the signal is sent through a series of THRU ports (as it is in a daisy-chain configuration), **each additional THRU port adds more distortion to the signal**. Eventually the data in the MIDI signal can become so distorted that it no longer conveys the original messages. This will cause erratic behavior in the receiving instruments. (The maximum number of allowable instruments in a daisy-chain will vary with the particular devices used, but problems may begin to occur if more than three are connected in this manner.)

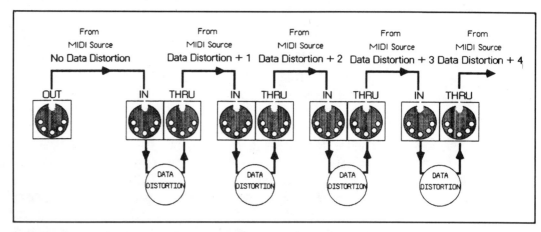

Each time MIDI messages are transferred through a MIDI THRU port, a slight distortion is added to the signal. The amount of distortion will vary from instrument to instrument.

When several instruments are interfaced via a series of THRU ports, each instrument adds more distortion to the MIDI signal. Although unnoticeable when using two or three instruments, the accumulated distortion may cause erratic responses when many instruments are interfaced using the daisy chain method shown above.

A MIDI THRU box can be used to eliminate or minimize this problem.

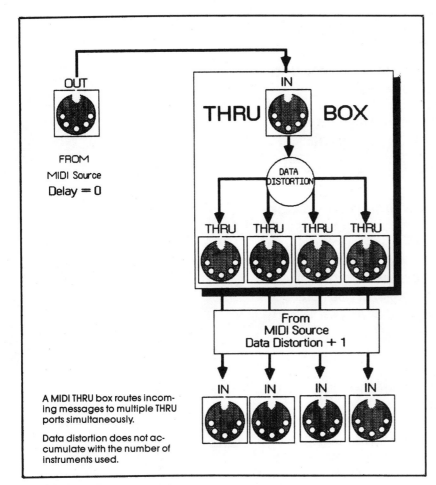

OUT

FROM
MIDI Source
Delay = 0

IN

THRU ● BOX

DATA DISTORTION

THRU  THRU  THRU  THRU

From
MIDI Source
Data Distortion + 1

IN  IN  IN  IN

A MIDI THRU box routes incoming messages to multiple THRU ports simultaneously.

Data distortion does not accumulate with the number of instruments used.

The simple solution to this problem is to use a MIDI THRU box. A THRU box has one IN port and multiple THRU ports. Since each of the THRU ports are connected to the same IN port, the **distortion** doesn't accumulate as it does when using a daisy-chain configuration.

By the way, a MIDI THRU box cannot be used to "mix" MIDI signals together, and they can't be combined with a "Y-cable." The digital words traveling the interface are very much like the trains we've been using for analogies. **Splicing** two MIDI cables together to combine two MIDI OUT signals would cause a disaster as surely as splicing two sets of railway tracks would. A microprocessor (or a Station Master) must be employed to oversee the timing of the two different outputs (or trains) before they could safely travel the same pathway. In MIDI terminology, the combination of two sets of MIDI messages is called a MERGE function.

## 2.5.0 SUMMARY OF THE MIDI INTERFACE

All in all, MIDI represents a powerful and flexible musical tool. Never before has it been possible to connect so many different musical devices together with a common interface. MIDI is the first interface that most musicians have ever used. Keep in mind that it is a **compound interface**. It can be used to send events and / or to synchronize timing between multiple MIDI devices. Events and the **timing reference** are carried by the same cables in a MIDI system. A lot of the confusion associated with using MIDI is a result of an unclear understanding of exactly what aspect(s) of MIDI are being transmitted/received by the instruments in a system.

## 2.5.1 MIDI Events

Two or more synthesizers connected together via MIDI transfer **events** (channel messages, etc.) **only**; so does a single sequencer connected to one or more synthesizers. A single sequencer requires no external timing reference; it uses its own internal Event Clock. The synthesizers only need event messages in order for them to play the sequence.

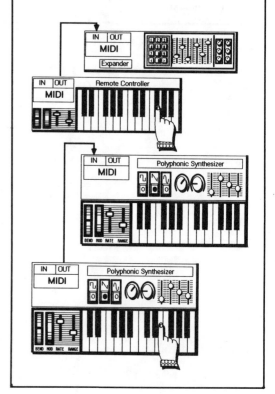

When interfacing two synthesizers, synthesizers and a single sequencer, or a remote controller and an expander, you are transmitting MIDI performance and operational event messages only.

In these situations, there is no need to provide the MIDI clock as a timing reference.

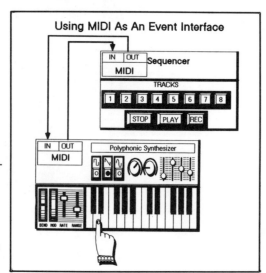

Using MIDI As An Event Interface

When two or more MIDI sequencers or drum machines are interfaced together, they must share a common timing reference. The interface keeps the drum and sequence rhythms synchronized with each other. The MIDI clock messages they share are like a metronome. They indicate where the beats (and sub-beats) fall. Clock messages carry no information about the actual notes or rhythms being performed.

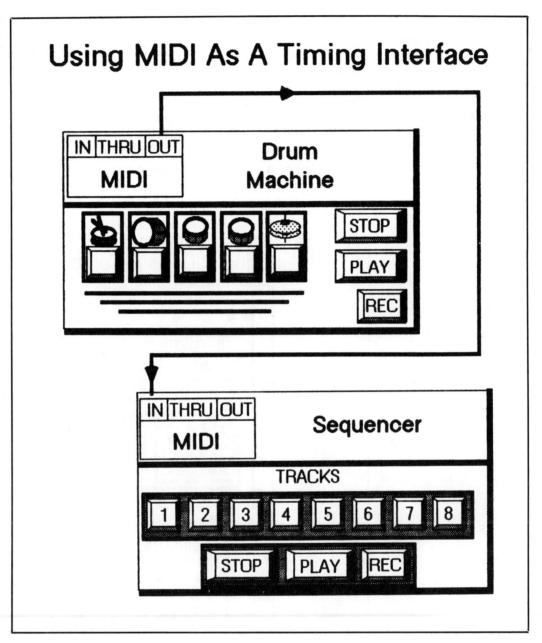

# Using MIDI As A Timing Interface

The MIDI clock is needed only when **two or more** sequencers, drum machines or arpeggiators are interfaced together. The MIDI clock is only used for synchronization. It does not have anything to do with what notes are played. It is used as a reference to indicate when events have occurred, or will occur.

Unlike the clocks used by non-MIDI devices, the MIDI clock signal is a binary code. It is sent over the same cable as all other MIDI messages at a rate of 24 clock messages per beat.

## 2.5.3 MIDI Events & Timing (Compound Interface)

In some situations it is necessary to transfer both timing reference and events together. For example, a sequencer could send events to a synthesizer and simultaneously be sending the MIDI clock to a drum machine via a MIDI THRU port. The synthesizer would **ignore** the timing messages and the drum machine would **ignore** the events messages.

In the real world, it is often necessary (or desirable) to use MIDI and non-MIDI instruments **together**. This means **two or more different interfaces must be used**. Typically, you will find it necessary to use a separate set of connections to transfer the timing reference between several non-MIDI and MIDI instruments. In the next section we will show you how to use MIDI effectively, as a single compound interface and in conjunction with non-MIDI interfaces as well.

When MIDI synthesizers, drum machines and sequencers are used together, it is not necessary to use separate cables for performance messages and the timing reference. MIDI is a true compound interface. Both performance messages and the MIDI clock are transmitted through a single cable.

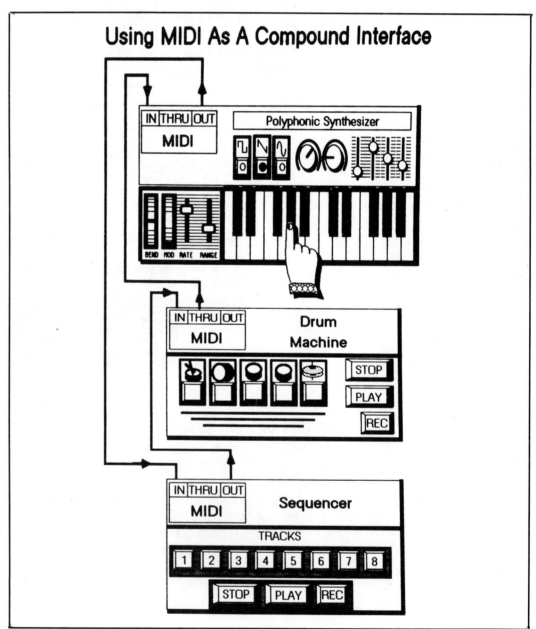

**Using MIDI As A Compound Interface**

# Section III:
# PRACTICAL APPLICATIONS
# OF MIDI INTERFACING

# 3.0.0 Practical Applications of MIDI Interfacing

If If you're like most people, you've come to this section first. You wanted to get right down to the meat of the matter so that you can start using your MIDI instruments intelligently. Good for you!

In this section we give you examples, tips, and pointers on how to use MIDI effectively. The details on why MIDI behaves the way it does, as well as the terms used to describe MIDI functions and messages, have been explained in the previous sections. If the terminology or theory isn't clear, don't panic. Just go back and read the sections you skipped.

If you have already read the previous sections, then you're ready to cruise through several examples of how to use what you've been reading about.

In either case, here you are. It is not possible to demonstrate every possible use of MIDI. One of the more exciting things about MIDI is that new uses of it are being developed almost every day. You will find that we've covered all of the basics and many more advanced applications as well.

## 3.1.0 Basic Interfacing: Synthesizer to Synthesizer

Let's start out simple and look at what's possible when interfacing two MIDI synthesizers together. Every MIDI instrument may implement a different subset of all possible MIDI features and functions. You must be able to evaluate an instrument's MIDI capabilities and their significance to your system as a whole.

We cannot stress the importance of owner's manuals enough. More often than not, they are the only source of information about a particular instrument's MIDI functions. Many times, the manual will also be the only source that explains how to access these functions from the synthesizer's controls.

While we're on the subject of manuals, we must point out that **not every** manufacturer uses the same terminology to represent the same MIDI features or functions. You may occasionally be required to perform a little detective work in order to figure out exactly what is being referred to in a manual. For example, the terms used to describe the MIDI modes are very carefully spelled out in the MIDI specification; yet not all manuals use these terms correctly. The formal definitions of the MIDI modes are:
*OMNI ON/POLY(Mode 1)*
*OMNI ON/MONO(Mode 2)*
*OMNI OFF/POLY(Mode 3)and*
*OMNI OFF/MONO (Mode 4)*

There are manuals that describe an instrument's MIDI modes as OMNI, POLY or MONO. Those words do not describe any of the four MIDI modes, so exactly what they are referring to is not clear. This type of confusion, though unfortunate, is a fact of life in the early stages of any industry standard. A **clear** and thorough understanding of MIDI is your defense against this confusion. In this book, we have made every effort to use the MIDI terminology cor-

# MIDI "Report Card" for Synthesizer Functions

**Synthesizer**

MANUFACTURER [ ]
MODEL [ ]

Here is a "report card" you can use to evaluate and compare MIDI implementations of different instruments. Make several copies of this chart and fill one out whenever you check out a new MIDI synthesizer. You'll find it makes it very easy to compare several different instruments at a glance to see how they "stack up."

**Polyphony**

6 VOICE ☐
8 VOICE ☐
12 VOICE ☐
16 VOICE ☐
OTHER ☐

**Modes**

| | YES | NO |
|---|---|---|
| 1 OMNI ON/POLY | ☐ | ☐ |
| 2 OMNI ON/MONO | ☐ | ☐ |
| 3 OMNI OFF/POLY | ☐ | ☐ |
| 4 OMNI OFF/MONO | ☐ | ☐ |
| BASE CHANNEL | [ ] | |

**Keyboard**

| | YES | NO |
|---|---|---|
| MIDI SPLITS | ☐ | ☐ |
| MIDI LAYERS | ☐ | ☐ |
| KEY NUMBERS | LO | HI |
| TRANSMIT | ☐ | ☐ |
| RECOGNIZE | ☐ | ☐ |

**Dynamics**

| | TRANSMIT | RECEIVE |
|---|---|---|
| ATTACK VELOCITY | ☐ | ☐ |
| RELEASE VELOCITY | ☐ | ☐ |
| CHANNEL PRESSURE | ☐ | ☐ |
| POLY KEY PRESSURE | | |

**Bender**

| | YES | NO |
|---|---|---|
| BEND AMOUNT ADJUSTABLE? | ☐ | ☐ |
| TRANSMIT | ☐ | ☐ |
| RECEIVE | ☐ | ☐ |
| ENABLE/DISABLE | ☐ | ☐ |

**Controllers**

| | CONTROLLER NUMBER | ASSIGNABLE YES | NO |
|---|---|---|---|
| CONTINUOUS | | | |
| MOD WHEEL | 1 | ☐ | ☐ |
| 1 | ☐ | ☐ | ☐ |
| 2 | ☐ | ☐ | ☐ |
| 3 | ☐ | ☐ | ☐ |
| 4 | ☐ | ☐ | ☐ |
| SWITCHES | | | |
| SUSTAIN | 64 | ☐ | ☐ |
| 1 | ☐ | ☐ | ☐ |
| 2 | ☐ | ☐ | ☐ |
| 3 | ☐ | ☐ | ☐ |
| 4 | ☐ | ☐ | ☐ |

**Program Change**

| | YES | NO |
|---|---|---|
| TRANSMIT | ☐ | ☐ |
| RECEIVE | ☐ | ☐ |
| ENABLE/DISABLE | ☐ | ☐ |
| NUMBER OF PRESETS | [ ] | |

rectly. All MIDI definitions and conventions, as well as the names of all MIDI messages and modes, are taken directly from the "MIDI 1.0 Specification." The MIDI definitions contained in Section II can be used as a master reference whenever ambiguous terms or definitions are encountered.

When you are checking out the MIDI functions of a particular instrument, here are the main things to look out for:

1. Does the instrument support more than one of the four MIDI modes? If so, which ones?

2. What Channel Voice Messages can it transmit/receive? In particular, does it recognize MIDI dynamics, pitch bend, modulation, etc.?

3. Can any MIDI messages be selectively enabled or disabled?

4. If the synth has clock-dependent features such as an onboard arpeggiator or sequencer, can they be synchronized to an external MIDI clock?

Many manufacturers supply a *MIDI Implementation Chart* with their products. The chart will give you most of the information you need to evaluate an instrument's MIDI features. We've given you an example of a typical implementation chart (with some tips on how to read it) and we've also provided a MIDI "Report Card" you can use for comparison of different instruments.

# Example MIDI Implementation Chart

| Function | | Transmitted | Recognized | Remarks |
|---|---|---|---|---|
| Basic Channel | DEFAULT | 1 | All Channels | WHEN FIRST POWERED UP, THE SYNTH TRANSMITS ON CH 1 AND RECEIVES ON ALL CHANNELS. THE RECEIVE AND TRANSMIT CHANNELS CAN BE SET TO ANY OF THE 16 MIDI CHANNELS BY THE USER. |
| | CHANGED | 1-16 | 1-16 | |
| Mode | DEFAULT | 1 | | WHEN POWERED UP, THE SYNTH IS IN MODE 1 (OMNI ON/POLY). IT TRANSMITS NO MODE MESSAGES, BUT IT WILL RECOGNIZE MESSAGES TELLING IT TO CHANGE TO ANY OF THE FOUR MODES. |
| | MESSAGES | X | 1, 2, 3, 4 | |
| Note Number | | 36-96 | 0-127 | THE SYNTH TRANSMITS NOTES OVER A 5 OCT. RANGE FROM ITS OWN KEYS. IT RECOGNIZES ANY VALID KEY NUMBER, BUT NOTES BEYOND 21-108 ARE SHIFTED IN OCTAVES TO FALL INSIDE THIS RANGE. THIS COINCIDES WITH THE 88 NOTES OF A GRAND PIANO. |
| | TRUE VOICE | -------------- | 21-108 | |
| Velocity | NOTE ON | 0 | 0 | ATTACK VELOCITY IS SENT AND RECOGNIZED. RELEASE VELOCITY IS NOT SENT AND IS IGNORED IF RECEIVED. NOTE ON/ATTACK VELOCITY =0 (9nH V=0) IS USED AS A NOTE OFF MESSAGE |
| | NOTE OFF | X 9nH V=0 | X | |
| After Touch | POLY | X | X | POLYPHONIC KEY PRESSURE MESSAGES ARE NOT SENT AND IGNORED IF RECEIVED. CHANNEL PRESSURE MESSAGES ARE TRANSMITTED AND RECOGNIZED. |
| | CHANNEL | O | O | |
| Pitch Bender | | * | * | PITCH BENDER MESSAGES ARE SENT AND RECOGNIZED. |
| Control Change | Modulation 1 | * | * | THESE CONTROL CHANGES CAN BE SELECTIVELY SENT AND OR RECOGNIZED. THE NUMBERS INDICATE THE CONTROL NUMBER DATA USED FOR EACH MESSAGE. |
| | Foot Control 4 | * | * | |
| | Foot Switch 65 | * | * | |
| Program Change | | 0-31 | 0-127 | 32 PROGRAM CHANGE MESSAGES ARE TRANSMITTED. RECEIVED MESSAGES BEYOND THE RANGE OF 0-31 ARE "WRAPPED AROUND" INTO THIS RANGE. |
| | TRUE # | -------------- | 0-31 | |
| System Exclusive | | * | * | CHECK YOUR MANUAL TO FIND WHAT EXCLUSIVE MESSAGES ARE SENT AND ACTED UPON. |
| System Common | SONG POS | X | X | NO SYSTEM COMMON COMMANDS ARE SENT OR RECOGNIZED. |
| | SONG SEL | X | X | |
| | TUNE | X | X | |
| System Real Time | CLOCK | X | X | MIDI CLOCK IS NOT SENT OR RECOGNIZED. |
| | COMMANDS | X | X | NO REAL TIME COMMANDS ARE SENT OR RECOGNIZED. |
| Auxiliary Messages | LOCAL ON/OFF | X | O | LOCAL ON/OFF IS NOT SENT, BUT IS RECOGNIZED. THERE ARE FIVE WAYS OF SPECIFYING AN ALL NOTES OFF MESSAGE (BY USING RESERVED CONTROLLER NUMBERS 123-127). ALL FIVE ARE RECOGNIZED AND NUMBER 123 IS TRANSMITTED. ACTIVE SENSING AND RESET ARE NOT SENT OR RECOGNIZED. |
| | ALL NOTES OFF | O (123) | O (123-127) | |
| | ACTIVE SENSE | X | X | |
| | RESET | X | X | |

Notes:
Mode 1: OMNI ON/POLY   Mode 2: OMNI ON/MONO         O : Yes       * : can be selectively
Mode 3: OMNI OFF/POLY  Mode 4: OMNI OFF/MONO        X : No              enabled/disabled

Here is an example of how a typical MIDI Implementation Chart for a keyboard instrument might look. The comments in the REMARKS column are more detailed than what you will find on an actual chart. Use them as a guideline for interpreting other MIDI implementations.

### 3.1.1 Responses to Channel Mode Messages

Three MIDI modes - OMNI ON/POLY (Mode 1), OMNI OFF/POLY (Mode 3) and OMNI OFF/MONO (mode 4) - are the building blocks to a MIDI system. OMNI ON/MONO (Mode 2) is not commonly used (see Section II, Channel Mode Messages). Don't worry if an instrument can't function in this mode.

When they are first turned on, all polyphonic MIDI keyboards should automatically go to the OMNI ON/POLY mode. This is the most basic mode. The instrument will respond to any channel message regardless of its channel assignment. If this is the only mode the instrument supports, then it will trans-

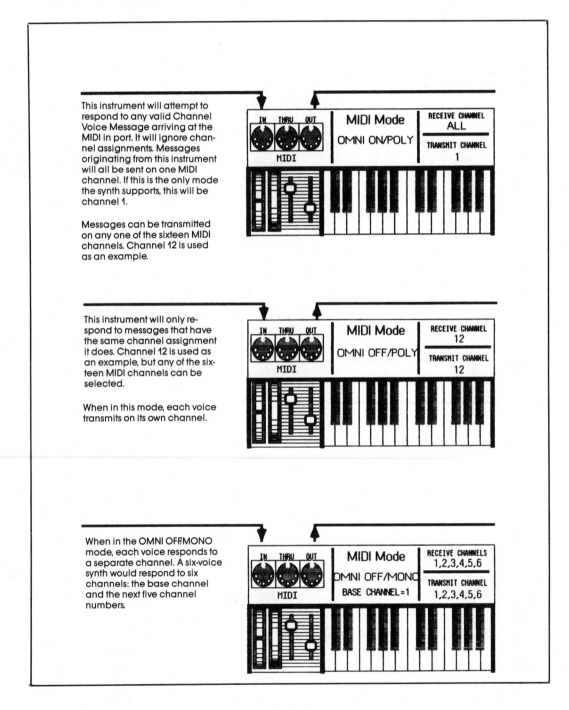

This instrument will attempt to respond to any valid Channel Voice Message arriving at the MIDI in port. It will ignore channel assignments. Messages originating from this instrument will all be sent on one MIDI channel. If this is the only mode the synth supports, this will be channel 1.

Messages can be transmitted on any one of the sixteen MIDI channels. Channel 12 is used as an example.

MIDI Mode OMNI ON/POLY — RECEIVE CHANNEL ALL / TRANSMIT CHANNEL 1

This instrument will only respond to messages that have the same channel assignment it does. Channel 12 is used as an example, but any of the sixteen MIDI channels can be selected.

When in this mode, each voice transmits on its own channel.

MIDI Mode OMNI OFF/POLY — RECEIVE CHANNEL 12 / TRANSMIT CHANNEL 12

When in the OMNI OFF/MONO mode, each voice responds to a separate channel. A six-voice synth would respond to six channels: the base channel and the next five channel numbers.

MIDI Mode OMNI OFF/MONO BASE CHANNEL = 1 — RECEIVE CHANNELS 1,2,3,4,5,6 / TRANSMIT CHANNEL 1,2,3,4,5,6

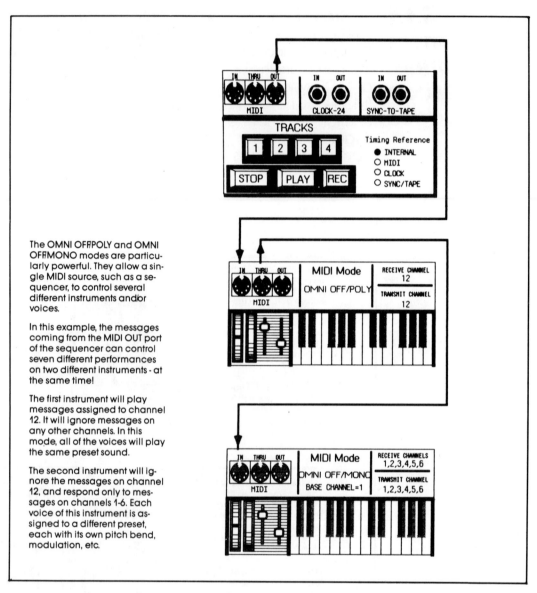

The OMNI OFF/POLY and OMNI OFF/MONO modes are particularly powerful. They allow a single MIDI source, such as a sequencer, to control several different instruments and/or voices.

In this example, the messages coming from the MIDI OUT port of the sequencer can control seven different performances on two different instruments - at the same time!

The first instrument will play messages assigned to channel 12. It will ignore messages on any other channels. In this mode, all of the voices will play the same preset sound.

The second instrument will ignore the messages on channel 12, and respond only to messages on channels 1-6. Each voice of this instrument is assigned to a different preset, each with its own pitch bend, modulation, etc.

mit on channel 1. If it supports other modes, it may transmit on another channel when first turned on.

OMNI OFF/POLY allows you to assign the instrument to one of the sixteen MIDI channels. All of its voices are assigned to the same preset sound. If the instrument can assign voices polyphonically, as in keyboard splits or layers, check to see if a separate MIDI channel can be assigned to each group of voices. This turns your instrument into multiple polyphonic synthesizers. If this is the case, be sure to check out how the instrument's controllers work with the MIDI split. For example, do they effect both splits (and their assigned MIDI channels) or can they be assigned to control one side of the keyboard and/or the other?

The OMNI OFF/MONO mode will only be available on instruments that can assign each voice to a different preset. In this mode a separate MIDI channel is assigned to each voice, turning each voice into an independent monophonic synthesizer.

## 3.1.2 Responses to Channel Voice Messages

MIDI defines a total of 128 different keys. That's more than ten octaves! A MIDI instrument does not have to have 128 keys to play 128 different pitches. For example, when the 88-note keyboard of instrument A is used to control instrument B, B will simply play the pitches, as if its keyboard had the same number of keys. Some instruments shift the notes in octaves until they fall within the instrument's keyboard range.

Channel Voice Messages are used to communicate performance events between instruments. These messages convey such information as which keys are played, the position of the pitch bender, etc. (see Section II, MIDI Defined, for a complete description of these messages). You can take it for granted that a MIDI instrument will transmit NOTE ON and NOTE OFF messages, **but other messages used for dynamics, control changes, and program changes, are not necessarily sent or received**. How do you find out? You've got it ; it's in the manuals! Here is what you need to know about the way MIDI instruments handle these various messages:

### Keyboard Ranges

Not all instruments have the same number of keys. Typical keyboard sizes vary between three and six octaves. What happens when two instruments with different size keyboards are interfaced with MIDI? There are two ways that an instrument can respond when it receives NOTE ON messages that are outside of its keyboard range. It will either play the notes with their proper pitches, or shift them in octaves until they are within the instrument's keyboard range. If an instrument shifts notes in this manner, its implementation chart shows the actual range of notes as "TRUE PITCH."

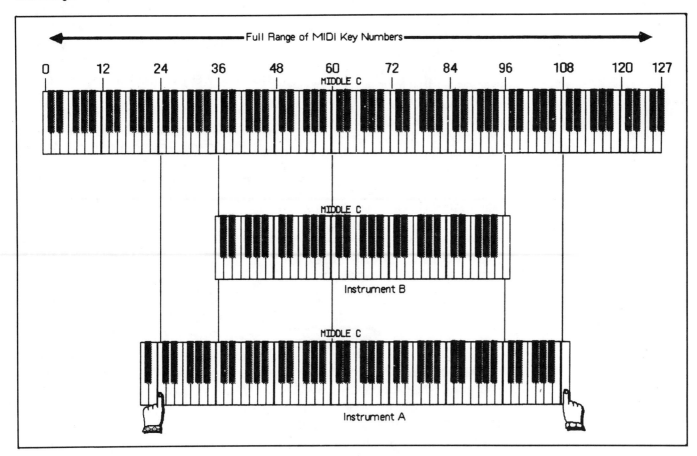

### Keyboard Transposition

Many instruments can transpose their keyboard ranges by one or more octaves. Some can transpose them by chromatic intervals. These transposition functions may or may not be transmitted via MIDI. The only way to know for sure is to check in the manual.

### Polyphony

Not all synthesizers contain the same number of internal voices. Eight-, six-, and sixteen-voice instruments are quite common. What happens when an instrument receives NOTE ON messages for chords with more notes than the instrument has voices? Such a situation could occur if you played a ten-note chord on a Yamaha DX7 (16 voices) that was controlling an Oberheim Matrix Six (6 voices). The Matrix Six would simply ignore the messages for the four "extra" notes, in exactly the same way it would if you played a ten-note chord on its own keyboard. Some newer instruments offer special *expansion* or *spill-over* modes. They can be used to actually increase the polyphony available from a given master keyboard. For instance, two six voice instruments can be used to create 12 note polyphony. These special modes are not MIDI modes (but the MIDI interface makes them possible).

### Dynamics

Most velocity-sensitive instruments only transmit Attack Velocity. A MIDI keyboard may also transmit a Release Velocity (if the synthesizer's keyboard is capable of sensing it).

There are two MIDI messages associated with pressure sensitivity: CHANNEL PRESSURE and POLYPHONIC KEY PRESSURE (see Section II, Optional Channel Voice Messages). CHANNEL PRESSURE is the most typical. A common After Touch value is applied to **all voices** in a channel. (This is how pressure sensitivity works on the Yamaha DX7.) Instruments that use POLYPHONIC KEY PRESSURE (Sequential Circuits T-8, Yamaha DX1) transmit a **separate** After Touch value for **each key held down**.

If an instrument can transmit a particular dynamic keyboard message, it is a safe bet that it will be able to receive them as well. Some **newer instruments** will respond to dynamic messages even if they cannot transmit them. However, the general rule of thumb is this: Using a dynamic keyboard instrument to control a nondynamic one will not make the second instrument dynamic. Every note of the second instrument will sound the same, no matter what kind of "touch" is used on the first keyboard. You can use a nondynamic keyboard to control a dynamic one; the second keyboard will play the notes with no dynamics (see Section II: Examples of Channel Voice Messages).

### Pitch Bending

You can be reasonably sure that a MIDI instrument will send and receive PITCH BENDER CHANGE messages. Check to see if pitch bending can be enabled/disabled, and if the amount of bend is adjustable.

When you use the pitch bender (whether it's a knob, wheel, or lever), it is essential to understand that the message it sends conveys its **position**, not pitch information. The amount of bend associated with a particular position is determined by the receiving instrument (see Section II, Examples of Channel Voice Messages). Problems arise if two instruments do not interpret the same physical position of the bender as the same musical instrument. When this happens, bending goes out of tune. If two instruments don't bend the same amount when interfaced via MIDI, here are your options for dealing with the situation:

* If the amount of bend is not adjustable on either instrument, you're stuck. Either don't use bend at all, or get into dissonance.

* If only one has an adjustable bend amount, set it to the same interval as the one that can't be adjusted. You are limited to this one interval, but the bending will be in tune.

* If the bend range of both instruments can be adjusted, you have the freedom to set them to any interval you want. As long as both intervals are the same, the bends will be in tune.

## Using Other Controllers

There is room within MIDI to be able to transmit/receive up to 64 additional controller messages. These could be used, for example, to convey mod wheel, breath controller, and foot pedal changes. Just **because a MIDI instrument has a mod wheel, don't assume that it will transmit messages when you move it**. It is up to the manufacturer to decide which controllers, if any, will transmit MIDI messages. This vital information is contained in the manual, and while you're checking to see if a controller is MIDI compatible, check to see what control number the manufacturer has assigned to it.

Standard practice is to assign the mod wheel to controller #1 and the sustain pedal to controller #64. There are some guidelines for other controller assignments (see Section II - MIDI In The Real World, for a chart showing common controller assignments).

You can assume that the one manufacturer will use the same MIDI controller numbers for the same controller on different instruments. However, different manufacturers don't always use the same controller numbers. More and more instruments are making the controller numbers assignable by the user. This is by far the most flexible way of dealing with the situation.

## Changing Presets

PROGRAM CHANGE messages are used to access different preset sounds. Remember, these messages have nothing to do with the actual sound parameters. They simply contain the number of a preset (0-127). Check to see if your instruments can send and receive these messages. You may not always want to change presets on all of your synthesizers at once; find out if this feature can be *enabled/disabled*.

If you do want to make simultaneous program changes, it's worth taking the time to organize your presets so that they work together. There is a chart in Section II that explains how instruments with dissimilar numbering systems will respond to program change messages. You will find that some presets sound great when they are used together. In fact, you might want to start to think of your interfaced MIDI synthesizers as one giant instrument.

## 3.1.3
## The Interface That Devoured Belleville (Applications)

Funny thing about MIDI: Once you realize that you can interface several independent instruments together to make one monster synthesizer, you get this feeling of incredible power...

**("Fools! I'll show them all. Igor, quick! More MIDI cables!! It's alive I tell you! ALIVE!!!)**

Like many a mad genius in the past, you can create something new from a collection of assorted pieces that you have lying around. By combining these pieces to make a single unit, you may be able to breathe new life into some old synths. Just don't get carried away, or a mob of noisy villagers will show up at your studio, waving torches and carrying dangerously rusted farm implements.

Here are some examples of how to use multiple synthesizers together with MIDI. You can use either the OMNI ON/POLY or OMNI OFF/POLY (make sure each synth is assigned to the same channel!) MIDI modes for each of these examples (refer to Section II for details). If you are interested in learning how to make the sounds mentioned here, or other synthesizer sounds, we recommend the SynthArts Video Instruction Course and text "Secrets of Analog and Digital Synthesis."

### Lead Sound With Feedback

Use MIDI to control Synth 2 from Synth 1's keys and controls.

When a note is played on Synth 1, at first you'll hear the guitar sound. As it fades out, a feedback tone from Synth 2 will slowly fade into the mix. Try tuning Synth 2 at different harmonic frequencies above Synth 1, such as an octave plus a fifth or two octaves.

For the best results, run the audio from the synths into a guitar amp or a high-quality distortion box.

### Feedback Guitar

Why is it that guitar sounds are so popular with keyboard players? Here's a way to get your favorite lead sound to "feed back." Although not complicated, this sound is not possible on most synths because it requires two sets of independent voices, but with MIDI and two instruments, it's a snap.

Get your favorite raunchy guitar sound on synth #1. Set the loudness envelope so that notes don't sustain, but smoothly fade to silence.

On synth #2, get a timbre that is as close to a sine wave as you can. Tune this sound an octave and a fifth above synth #1. Set the loudness envelope so that it smoothly crossfades with the guitar sound and then sustains.

Run the audio from both synths into a tube amp and crank it up. When you play, at first you will hear just your guitar sound (synth #1), but as you hold the key, that sound will fade and a feedback tone (synth #2) will build up behind it. For some variations, try tuning synth #2 to different harmonics, or controlling its level with different MIDI controllers.

## Articulation Dynamics With Non-Dynamic Keyboards

Here's a way to use a legato/staccato playing style as an alternative way to produce articulation dynamics from two non-dynamic keyboards. **Any two sounds could be used as long as they have envelopes similar to the ones described here**.

Set synth #1 to a bright percussive sound like vibes (quick attack and decay, no sustain). Add just enough release so that the notes "ring" slightly when you play staccato passages.

On synth #2 set up your favorite lush string sound. Make the attack fairly slow, so that when you play eighth notes you hear nothing. Tune this sound an octave below the vibes.

Your playing style, legato or staccato, will control the combined sound by bringing synth #2 in and out of the mix. Playing quick *staccato* passages will produce **only vibes** melodies. *Legato* passages will have a **string line** added an octave below. Try playing one-hand melodies and melodies against sustained chords.

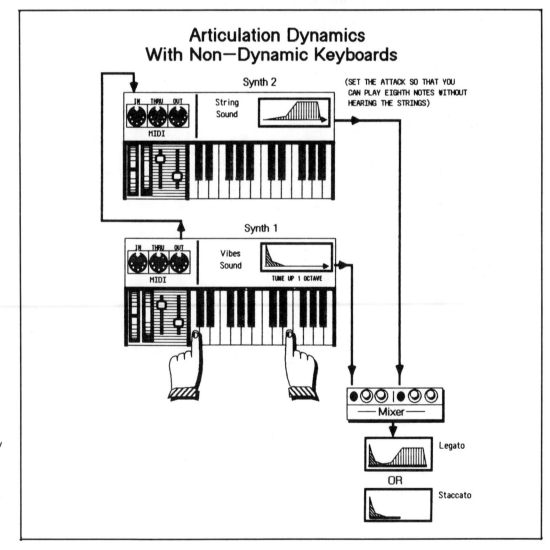

### Articulation Dynamics With Non—Dynamic Keyboards

Synth 2

String Sound

(SET THE ATTACK SO THAT YOU CAN PLAY EIGHTH NOTES WITHOUT HEARING THE STRINGS)

IN THRU OUT
MIDI

Synth 1

Vibes Sound

TUNE UP 1 OCTAVE

IN THRU OUT
MIDI

Mixer

Legato

OR

Staccato

The envelope settings are the key factors for this technique. A percussive vibes sound (quick Attack, no Sustain, slight Release) is used on Synth 1. Synth 2 has a string sound with a fairly slow Attack, maximum Sustain, and less Release than the vibes.

During quick staccato playing, only the vibes will be heard. Legato playing will produce both sounds.

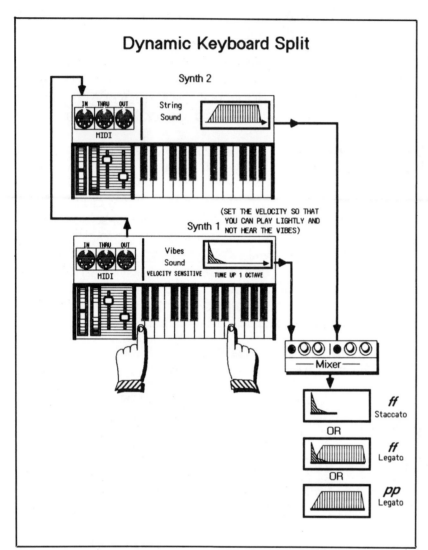

## Dynamic Keyboard Split

**Synth 2**

IN THRU OUT — String Sound

MIDI

(SET THE VELOCITY SO THAT YOU CAN PLAY LIGHTLY AND NOT HEAR THE VIBES)

**Synth 1**

IN THRU OUT — Vibes Sound

MIDI — VELOCITY SENSITIVE — TUNE UP 1 OCTAVE

Mixer

*ff* Staccato

OR

*ff* Legato

OR

*pp* Legato

In this variation, legato and staccato playing styles control the string sound, and keyboard dynamics control the vibes.

With a little practice, you can easily play just vibes, just strings, or both. You can freely split the two sounds anywhere on the keyboard - between either hand, or even each finger!

Any two sounds can be used, as long as their basic envelopes and dynamic sensitivity are the same as the ones shown here.

## Dynamic Keyboard Split

This is a variation of the above example. The same two sounds are used, but any sounds with similar envelopes will work as well. In this example, the combination of a dynamic keyboard controlling a non-dynamic one allows you to control which instrument will be played by which hand. With a little practice, you can control which instrument will be played by which finger!

On a velocity-sensitive keyboard, set up the vibes sound. Adjust the velocity so that you can play lightly on the keyboard **without hearing the vibes**. Use this instrument as the controller.

On the non-dynamic keyboard, set up the lush string sound again (you might not want to use as slow an attack as in the previous example).

This setup will let you turn either synth on or off with your playing style. **Hard staccato** will produce **only** the vibes sound. **Soft legato** playing will produce **only** the strings. **Hard legato will produce both**.

With a little bit of practice, you can easily play just vibes, just strings, or both. You can freely split the two sounds between left and right hands anywhere on the keyboard. Some interesting results can be obtained by tuning the two synthesizers to a non-unison interval.

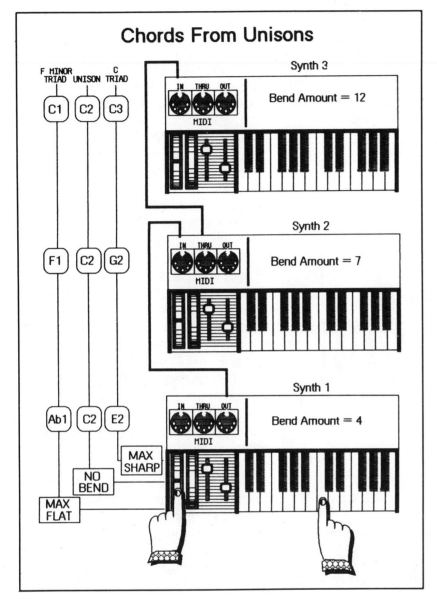

**Chords From Unisons**

F MINOR TRIAD — UNISON — C TRIAD

C1 C2 C3

F1 C2 G2

Ab1 C2 E2

MAX SHARP
NO BEND
MAX FLAT

Synth 3
IN THRU OUT
MIDI
Bend Amount = 12

Synth 2
IN THRU OUT
MIDI
Bend Amount = 7

Synth 1
IN THRU OUT
MIDI
Bend Amount = 4

## Chords From Unisons

**By no means feel that you must always pitch bend synthesizers in unison.** If you are lucky enough to have access to three MIDI synths, try this method of playing concerted voicings with non-unison bending.

Start off with three instruments tuned in unison. Any kind of sound will work. To begin with, try using the same kind of timbre on each instrument.

Set the pitch bend **amount** of the three instruments as follows: synth #1 - major third; synth #2 - fifth; and synth #2 - octave. While playing a C, moving the bender **all the way** up will change the relative tuning of the synths from unison to a **C-major triad** (second inversion). The note you're playing is the *root*. Moving the bender **all the way down** will change the relative tuning to an **F-minor triad** (third inversion). The note you're playing is the *fifth*.

Try it with the lead lines for a concerted "sectional" sound, or with simple chords to produce complex harmonic texture. Try changing the pitch bend intervals.

### *Altered Harmonies*

This is a really nice bender trick. It's easy to set up because only one synthesizer actually bends pitches. Using two synths, two fingers and the bender, you can create some very beautiful six-note voicings.

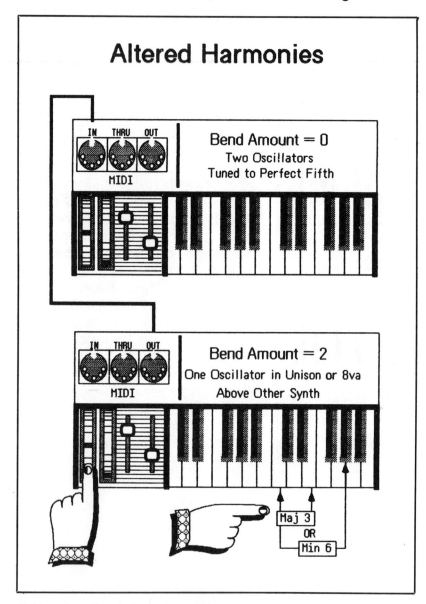

## Altered Harmonies

**IN  THRU  OUT**
MIDI

Bend Amount = 0
Two Oscillators
Tuned to Perfect Fifth

**IN  THRU  OUT**
MIDI

Bend Amount = 2
One Oscillator in Unison or 8va
Above Other Synth

Maj 3
OR
Min 6

In this configuration, playing major thirds or minor sixths will produce major seventh chords. Playing minor thirds or major sixths will produce minor seventh chords.

By sliding the bender to the maximum sharp position, a ninth and sharp eleventh will be added to the major seventh voicings, and a ninth and eleventh will be added to the minor seventh voicings.

Playing two keys produces six notes! Use any two sounds that blend well together. Be sure to experiment with different bender articulations.

On synth #1, set up a sound with two oscillators tuned in fifths. (When you play one key you hear that pitch, and another one a fifth above.) Set the pitch bend amount to 0 (no pitch bend). Control this synth from synth #2.

On synth #2, set up a sound that complements synth #1. Tune it to unison with the keyboard of synth #1. Adjust the pitch bend amount for synth #2 to a whole step.

The synth(s) tuned in fifths will play major and minor seventh voicings when you play two-note chords on the keyboard. *Major thirds* and *minor sixths* yield *major seventh chords.* You play C and E, you hear C, E, G and B. You play E and C, you hear E, B, C and G. Playing *minor thirds* and *major sixths* will yield *minor seventh chords.* You play C and E-flat, you hear C, E-flat, G and B-flat. You play E-flat and C, you hear E-flat, B-flat, C and G.

While holding down one of these two-note chords, slide the bender all the way sharp. You'll hear a *ninth* added to the above voicings. The C slides to D. You will also add an *eleventh* to the minor seventh voicings. The E-flat slides to F. A *sharp eleventh* will be added to the major seventh voicings. The E slides to F#.

Practice different kinds of bending techniques. (Hammer-ons and pull-offs work well.) Play a series of diatonic thirds in quarter notes while moving the bender up and down on the second and third beats of eighth-note triplets.

These basic Lydian and Dorian modal harmonies can be quite flexible, but try other two-note (or more) chords, different tunings, and different bender intervals.

## Experiment!

The above examples just barely scratch the surface in terms of the possibilities offered by a couple of MIDI synths and MIDI cables. MIDI can enhance the capabilities of your synthesizers, **but understanding MIDI won't necessarily make you a better synthesist**. The control and creation of musical sound is an art in itself. At the risk of appearing immodest, we would like to recommend (once again) the SynthArts products. Also, watch for new books from Ferro Technologies covering other aspects of MIDI and Music Technology.

Remember, intelligent use of MIDI functions and concepts can turn your individual instruments into components of one giant system. If you have thoroughly mastered the techniques of sound design utilized by each component, the giant will be under the control of your creativity. If not, your creativity will be hindered by the giant's complexity.

## 3.2.0 INTERFACING DRUM MACHINES AND SEQUENCERS INTO A MIDI SYSTEM

Drum machines and sequencers use internal Event Clocks as a timing reference (see Section I for details). When two or more of these devices are used together, they must be synchronized with a **common timing reference**. This is accomplished by interfacing them together so they may share a common Event Clock.

If all of the instruments involved are MIDI, hooking them up is quite simple. All MIDI instruments are compatible with each other. That is one of the advantages to having a standard interface. Complications arise if you must interface non-MIDI drum machines and sequencers with MIDI instruments.

Many of the popular drum machines and sequencers in use today were designed long before MIDI, and therefore don't have a MIDI interface. Chances are you will probably find yourself trying to interface dissimilar clock-based instruments together. This is not a major obstacle to overcome, but there are definite concepts and procedures you should be aware of.

## 3.2.1 Synchronization Basics

This chart compares the outputs of several common timing references used by drum machines, sequencers and synthesizers. Each of these clocks

There can be **one** and **only one** source of an Event Clock in a system. When interfacing drum machines and sequencers, the first thing you must do is decide which will be the *master*. This will be the **source** of the timing reference. All other instruments will be synchronized to it. On most instruments the Event Clock is labeled CLOCK, while on others it may be called SYNC. We use the term CLOCK when referring to the *electronic signal* used as a timing reference. We use the term SYNC only when referring to the *audio tone* used in conjunction with the SYNC-TO-TAPE function (see below).

It makes little difference if you use the drum machine or the sequencer to provide the master clock, but one must control the other. Once this decision has been made, you must determine if that clock is compatible with each of the other clock-based devices in the system. Here are the things you will need to know:

*Are the beat subdivisions of the master's clock the same as all of the other clocks it is controlling?

* Is the master's clock electronically compatible with all other clocks?

*Do any of the clocks require a RESET signal?

*Does the device you've selected as the master have a SYNC-TO-TAPE function? (You only need this if you want to synchronize with a tape machine.)

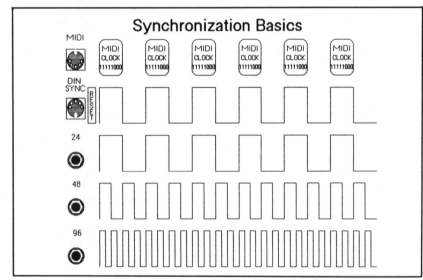

**Synchronization Basics**

divides a beat into a number of subdivisions. The equivalent to one 16th note (1/4 of a beat) is shown here. Each of these clocks is incompatible with the others.

The MIDI clock transmits a binary code 24 times per beat. These clock messages are sent in between performance messages, over the same MIDI cable.

The other clocks all use electronic signals (gates) to indicate beat subdivisions. The three most commonly used clocks divide a beat into 24, 48 or 96 subdivisions per beat.

A DIN SYNC clock also must transmit/receive a RESET signal before starting.

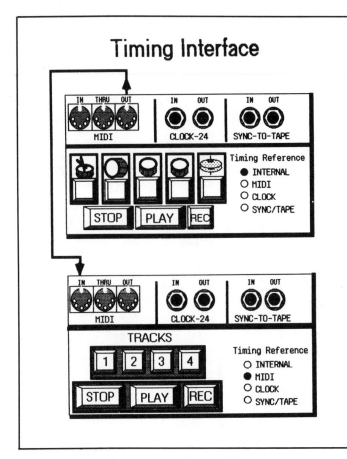

## Timing Interface

When two or more drum machines or sequencers are used together, one must be the source of the timing reference to all of the other devices. Remember, in this configuration event messages are not transferred, only the timing reference.

Most instruments provide more than one type of clock. Whichever one is used as the master clock source must be compatible with all of the other instruments in the system. Since MIDI is a standard interface, all MIDI clocks are compatible.

In this example, the drum machine acts as the "master." Its internal clock is transferred to the sequencer as MIDI messages via the MIDI OUT port. The sequencer uses the MIDI clock messages as a timing reference to keep its performance rhythmically synchronized with the drum machine.

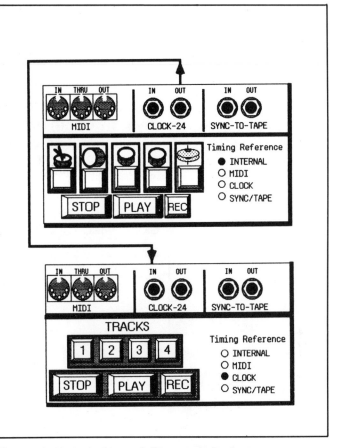

When an electronic clock is used as the source of the timing reference, the instruments must all use the same number of beat subdivisions. Many drum machines and sequencers allow you to select the number by giving you a choice between 24, 48 and 96.

In this example, the drum machine acts as the "master." Its internal clock is transferred to the sequencer as an electronic signal via the CLOCK OUT jack. The sequencer uses the signal as a timing reference to keep its performance rhythmically synchronized with the drum machine.

Notice that both instruments use the same number of beat subdivisions (24).

## Beat Subdivisions

*There are three common beat subdivisions* used by drum machines and sequencers: 24, 48 and 96 pulses per quarter note (see Section 1, Keeping Time). Many newer instruments allow the user to select any one of these three rates.

Most older machines use one fixed rate. The owner's manual will give you this information. Mismatched beat subdivisions **will cause** one instrument to play twice or four times faster than another.

75

## Electronic Compatibility

Sometimes, two instruments with the same beat subdivision won't work together because of electronic differences in their clock signals. **Jumpy, erratic rhythms (or no rhythms at all) are an indication of this kind of incompatibility**.

The timing reference used by MIDI is the MIDI CLOCK message. It is transmitted over the same MIDI cable as all other messages. The MIDI clock, which has 24 subdivisions per beat, will not work with other non-MIDI clocks with the same number of subdivisions. This is because the MIDI clock is transmitted as a binary code - not a series of gates, like other clocks.

When interfacing non-MIDI and MIDI drum machines and/or sequencers, it is common to use the non-MIDI clock as the timing reference. (Several examples of how this is accomplished are given below.)

It is often desirable to interface instruments with mis-matched clocks together. There are a number of commercially produced products that can be used to interface different types of clock-based instruments together. These examples show some typical clock interfacing configurations. The interface boxes are "generic" and are not meant to represent any particular product.

If you need such an interfacing unit, be sure to select one with the appropriate features and functions for your particular equipment.

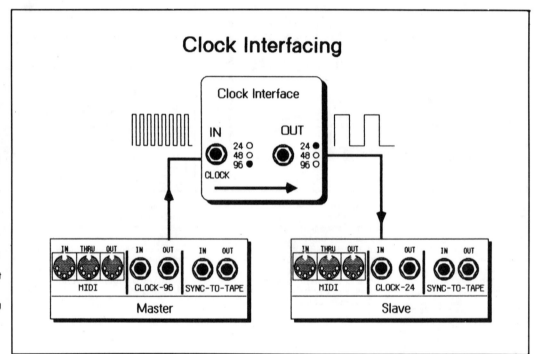

Clock Interfacing

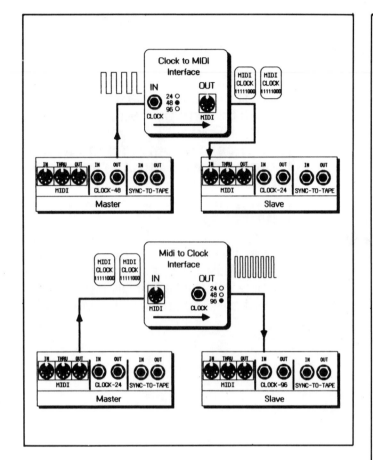

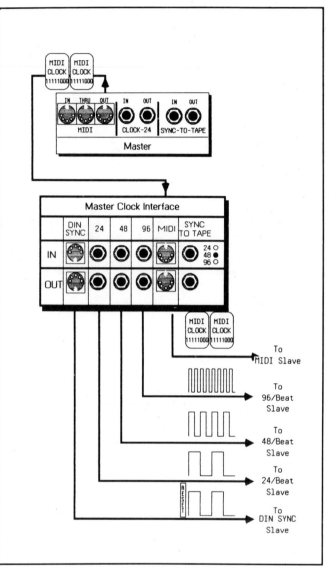

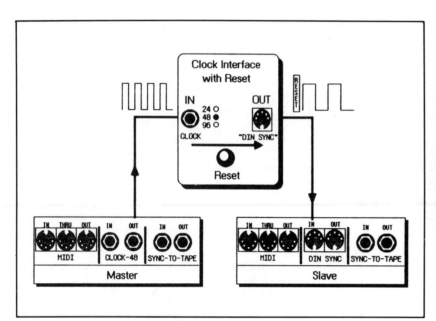

## RESET Signal

Some instruments require a RESET signal for their clocks. This signal ensures that the clock will start at the beginning of a cycle whenever the START button is pushed. An example of this is Roland's DIN Sync. **If your sequencer or drum machine slowly drifts out of time (a little more with each repitition of a loop or pattern), then it needs a RESET signal before it is started**.

By the way, although DIN Sync uses the same kind of connectors that MIDI instruments use, these are not compatible signals. Never connect a MIDI port to a DIN Sync jack.

## SYNC-TO-TAPE

It is possible to use a **track of a multi-track tape recorder** as the source of the timing reference. In order to do this, you must first record the timing reference onto the track. The SYNC-TO-TAPE function makes this possible. Tape recorders usually cannot record the clock signal directly from an instrument's CLOCK OUT jack. This is because clock signals don't transfer to and from analog tape accurately. The SYNC-TO-TAPE function converts the clock signal into an audio tone called a sync tone. The sync tone can be recorded accurately by any tape recorder.

Clock signals and sync tones are electronically **incompatible** with each other. The only time you will use the SYNC jacks is in conjunction with a tape recorder. SYNC OUT is used to send the sync tone to the tape machine. SYNC IN is used to send the sync tone from the tape machine back to the drum machine or sequencer.

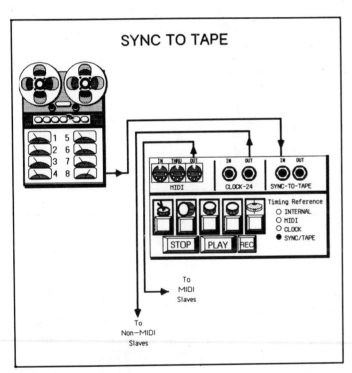

The SYNC-TO-TAPE function makes it possible to record the timing reference onto a track of a tape recorder. During playback, that track becomes the source of timing information to all clock-based instruments in the system.

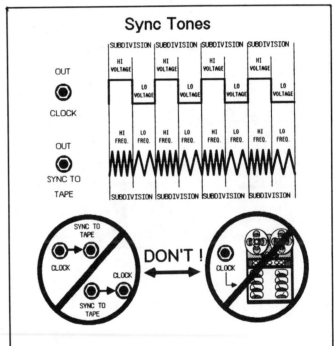

Clock signals alternate between a high and low voltage at a rate of one alteration for each beat subdivision. This kind of signal can not be recorded accurately by an analog tape recorder.

The SYNC-TO-TAPE function converts the electronic clock signal into an audio tone that can be recorded and played back by any tape recorder. There are several different methods used to convert clocks into sync tones. The most common is shown here. It is called an FSK tone (Frequency Shift Key).

Instead of alternating between a high and low voltage, an FSK sync tone alternates between a high and low frequency.

Sync tones and clock signals are not compatible with each other. Sync tones should only be used in conjunction with a tape recorder. Clock signals are used when interfacing directly with other instruments.

Here are some rules for using SYNC-TO-TAPE effectively:

1. Use the highest practical beat subdivision. This ensures accurate recording of the sync tone.

2. Make sure the tempo is set exactly where you want it. Once you record the sync tone, you can't change the tempo unless you record the sync tone again.

3. Pick an outside track to record the sync tone. Leave the adjacent track empty if possible. This minimizes cross-talk and "bleed" from the bias oscillator, which can distort the sync tone on playback.

4. Check your levels.

5. Record the sync tone alone, BEFORE anything else. If you record drums or the sequencer while recording the sync tone, they will be out of time with later tracks.

6. Record and play back direct. DON'T use any EQ, noise reduction, or limiting.

7. On playback, put the sync tone track in the OVERDUB SYNC or SIMUL SYNC mode.

8. Verify that your sync track works before you start recording subsequent tracks.

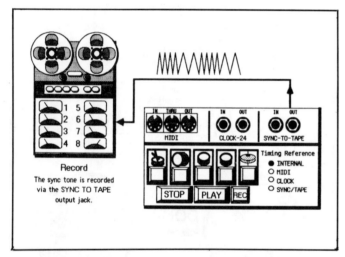

**Record**

The sync tone is recorded via the SYNC TO TAPE output jack.

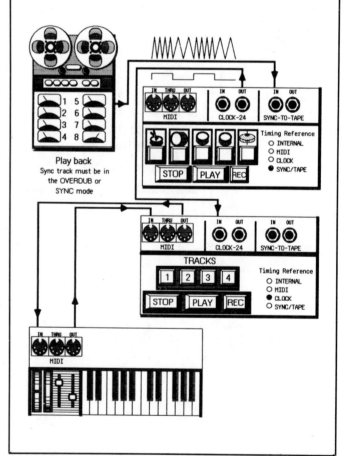

**Play back**

Sync track must be in the OVERDUB or SYNC mode

Guidelines for using SYNC TO TAPE correctly

1. Use the highest practical number of beat subdivisions.

2. Make sure the tempo is set exactly where you want it. Once the sync tone is recorded, the tempo can't be changed unless you re-record the sync tone.

3. Record the sync tone on an outside track. If possible, leave the adjacent track empty as long as you need to use the sync track.

4. Set the record level between 3 and 0 dB.

5. Record the sync tone alone, BEFORE anything else. Don't record any drum machine or sequencer parts while you are laying down the sync track.

6. Record and play back direct. Don't use any signal processing, noise reduction or limiting.

7. On playback, the track with the sync tone must be in the OVERDUB or SYNC mode.

8. Make sure the sync track works correctly before recording subsequent tracks.

Playback Sync track must be in the OVERDUB, SYNC or SIMUL SYNC mode.

## 3.2.2 Using MIDI Drum Machines

Most drum machines available now have some MIDI features. As with synthesizers, there are no rules about which features a drum machine must have to qualify as a MIDI instrument. You can expect a MIDI drum machine to have at least MIDI IN and OUT ports. Through these ports it can send or receive MIDI clock messages. The drum machine **may or may not** recognize other MIDI messages arriving at the IN port. (Time to get out the owner's manual again.) Here is a summary of the possibilities:

### Synchronization

In order to be compatible with a variety of MIDI and non-MIDI instruments, many MIDI drum machines provide more than one version of timing reference. Aside from the standard MIDI ports, a typical instrument may provide separate IN and OUT jacks for non-MIDI clocks, and SYNC-TO-TAPE. The non-MIDI clock usually offers a choice between 24, 48 and 96 beat subdivisions.

### MIDI Modes

* OMNI ON/POLY: The standard MIDI mode (see Section II). The drum machine will try to respond to all channel messages. It will transmit on one channel.

* OMNI OFF/POLY: In this mode the drum machine will receive/transmit on one user-assigned channel.

* OMNI OFF/MONO: In this mode each drum sound would receive/transmit on a different channel.

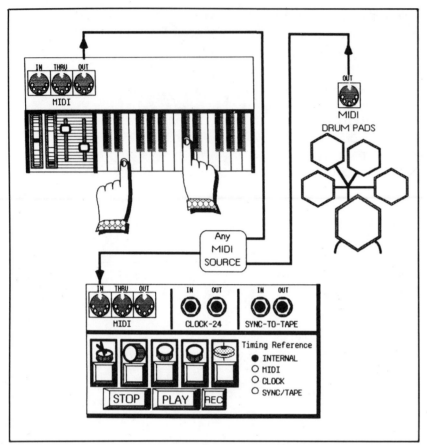

Many MIDI drum machines can be played by NOTE ON messages.

This makes it possible to control the drum sounds from any MIDI source such as: sequencers, keyboards, and MIDI drum pads.

Most of these machines will respond to the Attack Velocity data, which makes it very easy to program musical dynamics into drum patterns.

In this situation, MIDI is used as an event interface. (No timing reference is transferred.)

## Responses to Channel Voice Messages

At this time the only voice messages being utilized by drum machines are those related to simple keyboard performances. So far, no one has come up with a way to use MIDI Pitch Bend, Channel Pressure, etc., with a drum machine.

Many MIDI drum machines can be programmed from external MIDI controllers, such as keyboards or MIDI drum pads. NOTE ON messages from particular keys (or pads) will activate particular drum sounds. Some of these instruments will also respond to Attack Velocity data as well. This is a very musical way to program, or play, a drum machine. The owner's manual will have a chart that shows which sounds will respond to which keys.

Some of these instruments will transmit these NOTE ON messages as well. This makes it possible for one MIDI drum machine to "play" another. It could also be used to play a synthesizer. The possible pitches are limited by the number of drums, and the notes will have very short duration.

## Responses to System Common Messages

* SONG POSITION/Pointer Number: can be used to communicate a beat location (to the nearest 16th note) within a drum pattern or sequence.
* SONG SELECT/Song Number: may be used to select a preset drum pattern.

## Responses to System Real Time Messages

* MIDI CLOCK: As described above, this is the MIDI Event Clock, used by the system as a timing reference. It divides each beat into 24 subdivisions.
* START, STOP, CONTINUE: These are the messages used to control the operation of MIDI sequencers and drum machines.

## 3.2.3 Using MIDI Sequencers

A sequencer stores a list of performance-related messages referenced to an Event Clock (see Section I, Keeping Records). This list associated with a single performance is generally called a track. Many sequencers can divide this internal list into several *independent tracks*, each one associated with a different performance. These separate tracks can be layered to form multi-performance orchestrations, or linked end-to-end to create songs from small musical phrases.

Each track of a MIDI sequencer can record any Channel Voice Messages. This means that a single track of a MIDI sequencer could contain messages from up to sixteen MIDI channels, each channel controlling a separate synthesizer. We learned in Section II that these messages can describe many other aspects of a performance besides which notes were played. For example, a MIDI sequencer can record the messages associated with pitch bend, dynamics, mod wheel changes, and other controller changes as well. This ability makes MIDI sequencers very useful, but be aware that **every message** takes up a certain amount of space in the sequencer's overall memory. There is always a limit to how long a list the sequencer can store.

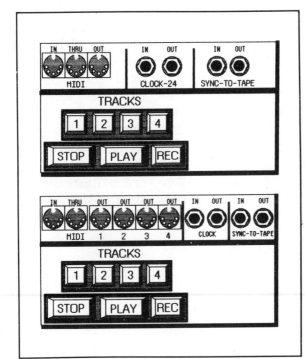

Each track of a MIDI sequencer can contain performance messages assigned to any combination of up to sixteen MIDI channels. Some sequencers route these messages to one MIDI OUT port. Such a sequencer can be used to control up to sixteen separate performances, one for each channel. More sophisticated sequencers have multiple MIDI OUT ports. These devices can control up to sixteen separate performances from each OUT port. Another (perhaps more practical) advantage of multiple OUT ports is that they allow you to send messages for separate channels through separate ports. This makes it possible to minimize the delays caused by transmitting large amounts of performance messages through a single port, as well as those delays caused by daisy chaining.

### Memory Allocation

One of the more important features of a sequencer is the size of its memory. Often, this is given as a number of notes. For example, a typical sequencer might be able to record 4,000 notes. What exactly is a "note," and how much memory space does it take up? There are no hard definitions, but it's safe to assume that a single note **would be defined by** the messages needed to describe a particular key depression and release. MIDI requires a minimum of two complete messages (NOTE ON and NOTE OFF) to describe a single note. Typically each message is 3-bytes long, so six bytes are needed to specify a single note. (Some devices can save a few bytes by taking advantage of a MIDI designed feature called "Running Status.") A 4,000-note sequencer therefore could probably record about 8,000 three-byte MIDI Channel Voice Messages. Remember, MIDI messages are not all the same length, so the total number of messages could vary quite a bit.

If you only play keys and don't use any other performance controls, that 4,000-note length is a good guideline for memory size. If you use other means of musical expression be aware that...

* Every **switch-related message** (caused by changing programs or using footswitches, etc.) takes up about the same amount of memory as **pushing down** a key on the keyboard.

* Nothing eats up memory faster than using continuous controllers. If you do a lot of pitch bending, for example, that 4,000-note limit might be more like 400 notes. Using **any continuous controllers** like the bender, mod wheel, after touch, etc., takes up a great deal of memory space. This isn't because their messages are very long. It is because a new message is sent whenever the controllers are moved, even if that motion is very slight. Sliding the bender up and down its range will transmit several hundred messages. Since the messages convey the controller's position (not pitch information), it doesn't matter what interval the bender is set for (see Section II). In other words, when you use a continuous controller, you are sending a continuous series of messages.

It is up to you to decide how you want to use memory. You can record more notes if you avoid using the continuous controllers, or you can have more freedom of expression if you are willing to sacrifice the total number of notes you can record. Some sequencers can filter out certain dynamic messages, leaving more room in memory for NOTE ON and OFF messages (see below).

If you try to use a sequencer like a tape recorder, you might be disappointed. You can never get as many notes into a sequencer as you can on a reel of 24-track tape. Use the sequencer as a compositional tool. **You don't have to record every single note of a tune from end to end**. Use loops, links and other sequencer tools to build compositions. You can build songs and arrangements by recording small patterns. The patterns can be combined to form larger pieces. Taking a **modular approach to composition** will free up more memory, giving you the freedom to record subtle performance dynamics, as well as notes.

## Synchronization

Most MIDI sequencers provide the same synchronization options as MIDI drum machines. Aside from the standard MIDI ports, there are usually IN and OUT jacks for non-MIDI clocks, as well as SYNC-TO-TAPE IN and OUT.

## MIDI Modes

* OMNI ON: In this mode the sequencer can record messages from any channel, or combination of channels, onto a single track.
* OMNI OFF: This mode allows the user to select which channel the sequencer will record on a track. All other channels will be ignored.
* On most sequencers, the channel assignment is fixed once a track is recorded. In other words, if track one recorded a synthesizer transmitting on MIDI channel 8, then that performance will remain assigned to channel 8 when track one is played back. The manual will tell you if you can reassign channels after they've been recorded onto tracks.

## Responses to Channel Voice Messages

As noted above, a MIDI sequencer can record all Channel Voice Messages, including PROGRAM CHANGE. In order to optimize memory allocation, many sequencers can be set to ignore certain meessages like CHANNEL PRESSURE, POLYPHONIC KEY PRESSURE, and PITCH BEND CHANGE. Some sequencers can be set to ignore the Velocity data associated with NOTE ON and OFF messages as well.

A useful feature on MIDI sequencers is called *echo*. (Not to be confused with the repetition of sound that is also called an echo.) This feature allows the messages arriving at the sequencer's MIDI IN port to be transferred to its MIDI OUT port, making it possible to play MIDI slaves directly from the keyboard when the sequencer is not playing.

Without this feature, it is necessary to physically disconnect the slaves from the sequencer's OUT port and reconnect them to its THRU port (since the OUT port of a MIDI device doesn't normally transmit messages arriving at the device's IN port).

## Responses to System Common Messages

These messages are not recorded by the sequencer. They are used to convey operational information only.

* SONG POSITION/Pointer Number: is used to communicate a location (to the nearest 16th note) within a sequence.
* SONG SELECT/Song Number: is used to select one of 100 possible preset sequences.

## Responses to System Real Time Messages

* MIDI CLOCK: As described above, this is the MIDI Event Clock. It is used by the system as a timing reference. It subdivides each beat into 24.
* START, STOP, CONTINUE: These messages are used to control the operation of the sequencer.

## 3.2.4 Interfacing Examples Using MIDI Drum Machines and Sequencers

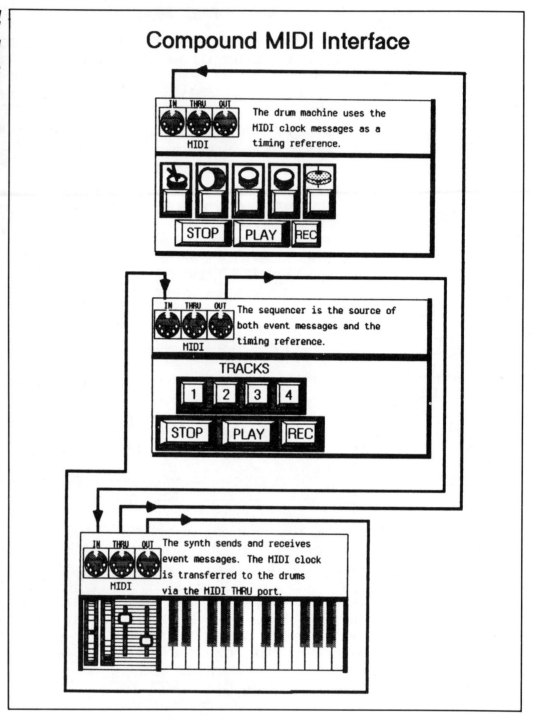

Compound MIDI Interface

The drum machine uses the MIDI clock messages as a timing reference.

STOP    PLAY    REC

The sequencer is the source of both event messages and the timing reference.

TRACKS

1  2  3  4

STOP    PLAY    REC

The synth sends and receives event messages. The MIDI clock is transferred to the drums via the MIDI THRU port.

Some MIDI drum machines and sequencers only provide MIDI ports for interfacing.

In this instance, MIDI is used to transfer both event messages as well as the MIDI clock as a timing reference.

# Compound Interface
# With Non—MIDI Timing Reference

If your drum machines and sequencers give you the option of using a non-MIDI clock as a timing reference, it can be used instead of the MIDI clock messages.

This can help avoid the slight (but inevitable) delays caused by using MIDI THRU ports.

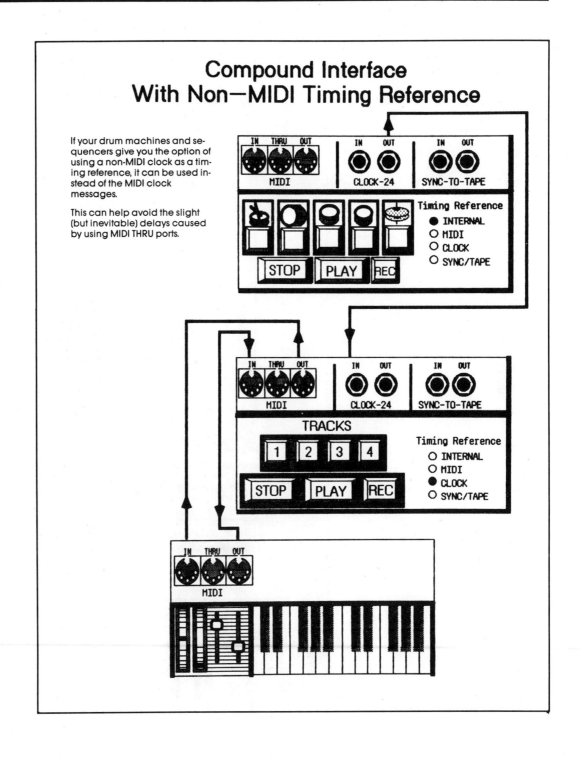

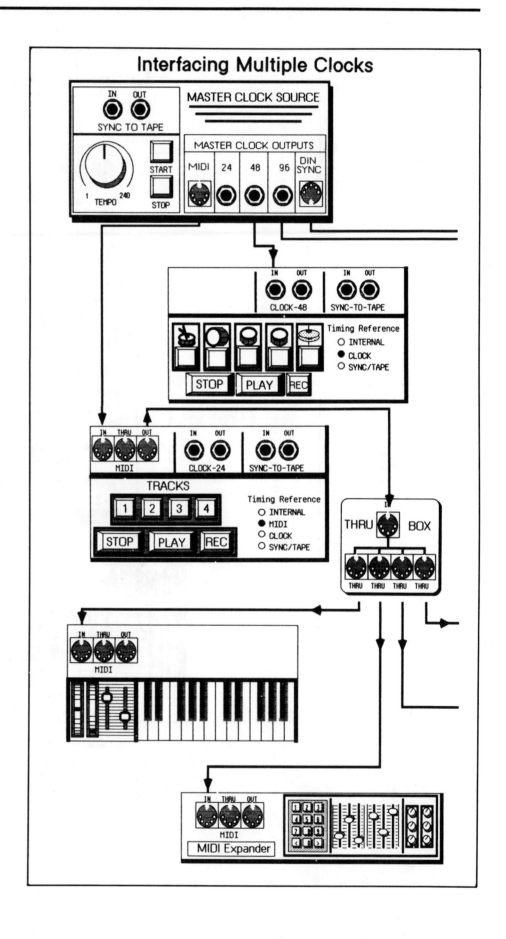

Interfacing Multiple Clocks

It is not uncommon to use several MIDI and non-MIDI devices together, especially in the studio. If several different kinds of timing references are required, a master clock source is an invaluable interfacing aid. Such a device can provide many different kinds of clock signals simultaneously, each one perfectly synchronized with the others. In this example, a single master clock is generating MIDI, DIN SYNC, as well as 48 and 96 subdivision clocks.

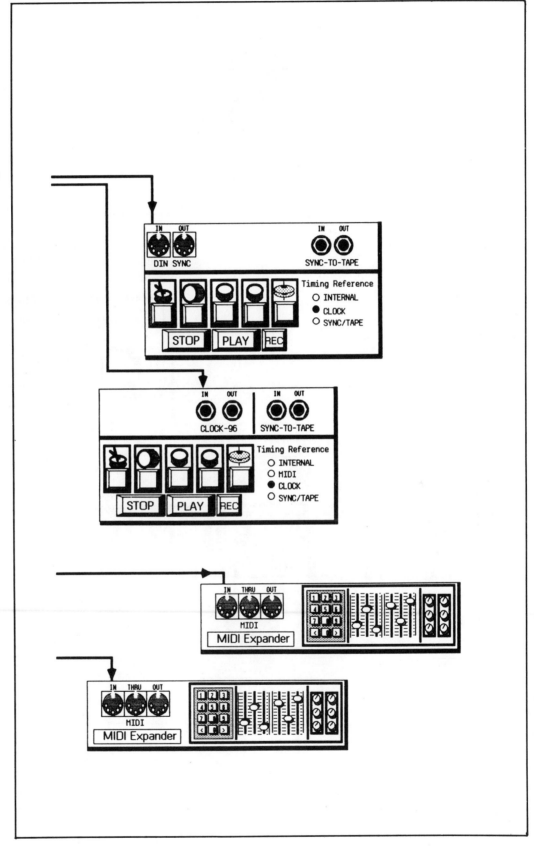

Several independent performances, each with its own preset sound, can be layered on tape with a single MIDI synth and a sequencer with SYNC-TO-TAPE.

Record each performance into the sequencer, changing the channel assignment of the synth each time.

Record the sync tone and connect it to the SYNC-TO-TAPE input.

Record the sequencer tracks as a series of overdubs. Change the channel assignment of the synth and the preset sound for each overdub.

The SYNC-TO-TAPE function will ensure that each performance is in time with the others.

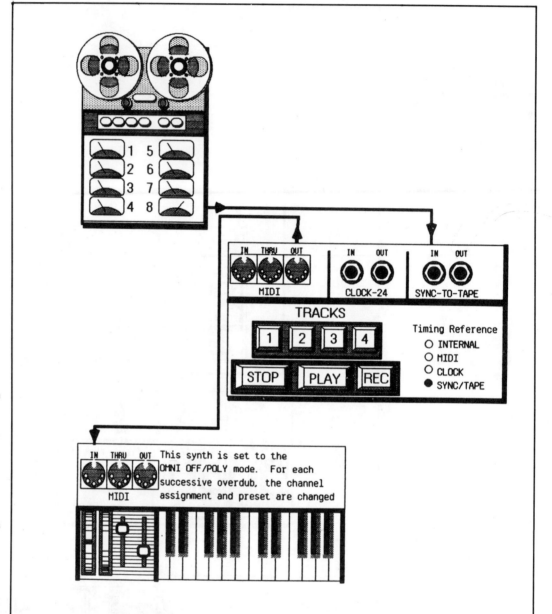

This synth is set to the OMNI OFF/POLY mode. For each successive overdub, the channel assignment and preset are changed

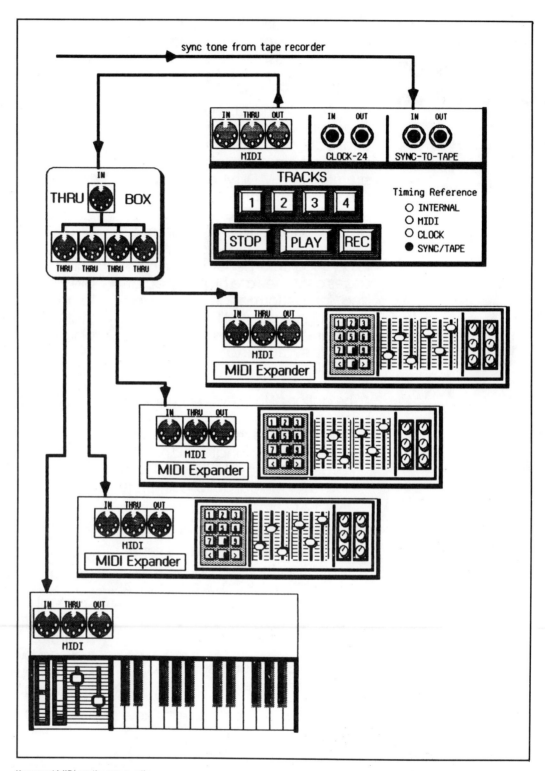

If several MIDI synths are available, each one can be set to a different channel and all of the sequencer tracks can be recorded onto the tape recorder at the same time.

## 3.3.0 CHOOSING A REMOTE CONTROLLER

The MIDI interface is making some profound changes in the way musicians can use their instruments. These changes are reflected in new products that have been designed with MIDI in mind. For example, specialized MIDI keyboards are available that are meant to be used as the main performance instrument of a MIDI system. They are used only to control other instruments, and have no sound-producing circuitry of their own. These remote controllers are meant to be a source of performance messages only. They are highly specialized for performance "feel" and meaningful use of MIDI functions. Here are some things to consider when evaluating a remote controller:

* The action of the keyboard should be one that fits your performance style. There are several variations, from the traditional organ-type keyboard to ones with weighted and mechanical actions simulating piano "feel."

* Whatever the action style, you want velocity and pressure sensitivity. Attack Velocity and Channel Pressure are the norm, but the addition of Release Velocity and Polyphonic Key Pressure is the ultimate in MIDI dynamics.

* The controller should support all of the MIDI modes.

* Look for features that allow the keyboard to be split into zones, each zone having its own MIDI channel or modes.

* If you use sequencers and drum machines in conjunction with your playing, you might want a controller that can transmit the START, STOP and CONTINUE messages. This makes it possible to control their operation from one central location.

* Aside from a MIDI PITCH BENDER, a remote controller should have several continuous controllers and switches that can be assigned to any of the 64 MIDI controller numbers. Even more desirable is the ability to assign controls to any MIDI parameter, including System Exclusive voicing parameters.

* It should be possible to call up MIDI preset sound numbers and song numbers from the controller.

* Each of the controller's settings, controller assignments, channel and mode assignments, preset numbers, etc., should be storable as a preset. This makes it possible to store and recall entire multi-instrument setups as simply as storing and recalling a single sound.

* An ideal remote controller would have multiple MIDI OUT ports to minimize the potential problems caused by daisy chaining. If not, then it should be used in conjunction with a MIDI THRU Box (see Section II).

## 3.4.0 Personal Computers and MIDI

Since MIDI is a digital interface, it is possible to use personal computers in conjunction with MIDI instruments. When MIDI was first introduced, this was the source of much excitement and speculation. In reality, this can become a source of confusion and frustration. The simple fact that you own both a MIDI instrument and a personal computer does not mean that the two devices will be able to work together. Remember, MIDI was designed to interface musical instruments. It was not designed to interface musical instruments directly with computers. There are two main considerations when using MIDI instruments with computers: hooking them up and software.

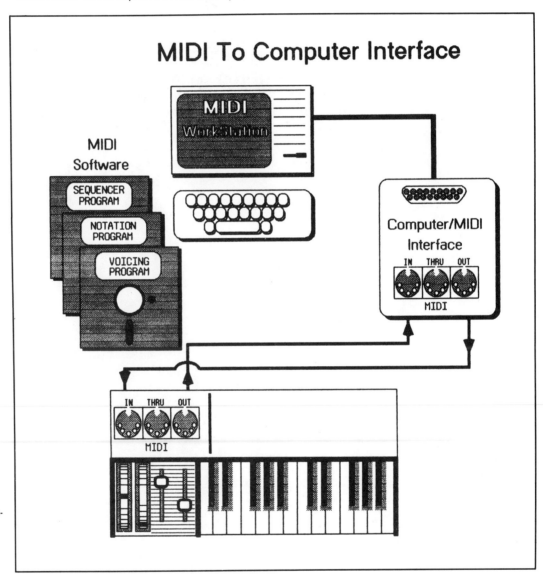

MIDI To Computer Interface

Most computers cannot be connected directly to MIDI instruments. A separate MIDI/COMPUTER interface is required.

### 3.4.1 Hooking Them Up

Most computers do not have a MIDI interface built into them. At this time, only the ATARI ST comes from the factory with onboard MIDI ports. The MIDI interface is **incompatible with standard computer interfaces**, like the RS232, so an additional MIDI/COMPUTER interface is needed in order to be able to transfer information between them. There are a number of commercially available interfaces available from Assimilation Technology, Roland, Passport, Hybrid Arts, and others.

If you are getting an interface, make sure it will work with your brand and model of computer.

## 3.4.2 Software

Once you have the interface between MIDI and your computer, you will not be able to do anything useful until you get some software. You must make sure that the software is compatible with your computer and interface.

Software, of course, is the heart of the matter. It is the software that will actually allow you to do whatever it is you want to do with your MIDI/computer interface.

### Commercially Available Software

MIDI software is a new phenomenon. There are many possible applications, and over the coming years a wide variety of innovative and useful products will be available. Right now, the first generation of MIDI software is centered around three areas:

*Voicing Programs: assist you in creating and organizing sounds on a particular synthesizer. They are not available for every synthesizer, but the variety is growing. These programs can be quite useful. Aside from making programming more efficient (not to mention more fun), they usually provide a means of storing sounds on a diskette. Disks are much cheaper and hold many more sounds than RAM cartridges.

* Sequencers: are among the most popular type of software. Their functions and uses will be similar to those of a stand-alone sequencer. In general, a software-based sequencer should have very sophisticated editing features, multiple tracks, and a large amount of message storage space. Be sure to evaluate the program to find out if it fits your needs.

* Music Notation Programs: use computer graphics to display standard musical notation. Most work by transcribing keyboard performances. Generally, these programs are not intended to produce publication-quality sheet music, but they can be helpful to a student or arranger.

### Writing Your Own Software

If you have experience programming your own computer, or if you want to learn, you can design and write your own MIDI programs. You will be pretty much on your own. There are not many references available to the MIDI programmer. However, in the near future, there will be more help available to persons interested in creating their own music software. As part of the Ferro Technology Series of Publications, there will be a book that deals with this subject. Look for it in the near future!